EMPOWERING HABITS

*How To Acquire Habits That Will
Lead You To Quickly
Reach Your Goals*

Marc Walker

© Copyright 2020 by Marc Walker.

All right reserved.

The reproduction, transmission, and duplication of any of the content found herein, including any specific or extended information, will be done as an illegal act regardless of the end form the information ultimately takes. This includes copied versions of the work both physical, digital and audio unless express consent of the Publisher is provided beforehand. Any additional rights reserved.

Furthermore, the information that can be found within the pages described forthwith shall be considered both accurate and truthful when it comes to the recounting of facts. As such, any use, correct or incorrect, of the provided information will render the Publisher free of responsibility as to the actions taken outside of their direct purview. Regardless, there are zero scenarios where the original author or the Publisher can be deemed liable in any fashion for any damages or hardships that may result from any of the information discussed herein.

This is a legally binding declaration that is considered both valid and fair by both the Committee of Publishers Association and the American Bar Association and should be considered as legally binding within the United States.

Table Of Contents

Introduction	11
Chapter 1: Your Habits Drive Your Lifestyle	**15**
Everyone Has Unconscious Habits	16
Your Habits Drive Your Lifestyle	19
How Bad Habits Keep You In a Low Quality Life	22
How Good Habits Will Transform Your Life	25
The Eight Areas Of Your Life To Improve	27
Chapter 2: Quit Relying On Chance and Take Responsibility	**33**
Chance Is Not Worth Betting Your Life On	34
Extraordinary Events Don't Make Extraordinary People	38
Taking Responsibility For the Quality Of Your Life	41
Taking Responsibility For the Habits You Have Created	44
Identifying Damaging Habits You Have Been Holding Onto	47
Chapter 3: The Facts About Habits	**51**
What Is a Habit?	53
Where Are Habits Formed In the Brain?	56

How Long Does It Take To Form a Habit? 59
What Is the Benefit Of Habits? 61
Can We Live Without Habits? 64
Chapter 4: Three Step Habit Loops **67**
The Three Steps Of a Habit Loop 68
Step One: The Cue 70
Step Two: The Routine 73
Step Three: The Reward 76
The Anatomy Of a Strong Reward 78
Chapter 5: Diverting Your Desire **83**
Resisting Desire Creates Relapses 85
Identifying Your True Desire 91
Redirecting Your True Desire 97
Finding a Healthier New Routine 100
Remaining Conscious Over Your Desires 102
Chapter 6: Planning Your New Habits **105**
Identifying the Need For New Habits 106
The Anatomy Of a Positive Habit 108
Giving Your Reward Significance 113
Planning Out Your New Habit, Step-By-Step 115
Planning the Execution Of Your New Habit 118
Chapter 7: Executing Your New Habits **121**
Willpower and the Motivation To Engage 123
Turning Motivation Into a Habit 124
Forming Your New Habits Around Existing Ones 126

    Rewarding Yourself For Motivation   129
    Steps For Staying Consistent   132

Chapter 8: How To Pamper a Habit (and Why)   **137**
    Why New Habits Will Always Be More Fragile   138
    What Happens When You Don't Pamper a Habit   141
    What It Looks Like To Pamper a Habit   144
    How To Pamper Your Own Habit   147
    Being Mindful Of High Stress Periods   150

Chapter 9: Making Habits As Simple As Possible   **153**
    Effective Methods For Simplifying Your Habits   155
    How To Ensure That You Still Get Your Desired Results   158

Chapter 10: How To Break Bad Habits   **161**
    Getting Real With Yourself About Bad Habits   162
    Fitting a New Routine Over Your Habit   166
    Mindfully Navigating the Breakdown Of Your Bad Habit   169

Chapter 11: Habits You Should Have   **173**
    Getting Up Early Each Morning   175
    Giving Gratitude For Each Day   176
    Making a List Of Your Goals   177
    Exercising Daily   179
    Eating a Healthy Diet   180

Managing Your Money Properly	181
Keeping a Precise Agenda	182
Enjoying an Hour To Yourself	184
Checking In With Yourself Each Evening	185
Reading For 30 Minutes Before Bed	186
Chapter 12: Habits You Should Quit	**189**
Smoking	190
Biting Your Nails	192
Sleeping In	193
Leaving Late	194
Relying On Temptations	195
Saying "I'll Do It Later"	196
Not Taking Your Wellbeing Seriously	197
Spreading Negativity	199
Conclusion	**201**

Dedication

To my parents, who made it possible for me to acquire the habits that lead me to be a happy and successful person.

Introduction

Habits seem like a topic of common sense in our modern society, yet the actual reality of what habits are, how they work, and why they seemed to be something that very few people actually know about or understand. Instead, people realize that habits are things they engage in repeatedly and that produce certain wanted, or unwanted, results on a continuous basis. Often, people will make excuses for their habits, use habits to justify their behaviors, and otherwise act as though they are a victim of their habits. Of course, if you do not understand how habits work, this can feel incredibly true. That is because habits work on a deep, subconscious level within your mind, and they are designed to make engaging in repetitive behaviors easier. Once a habit is formed, your conscious mind and the majority of your brain, in general, is completely removed from the practice as it becomes an automatic behavior. This will happen regardless of whether or not the habit is positive or negative because, quite frankly, your brain does not care about that. All it cares about is creating the desired reward and making it effortless for you to experience that reward over and over again.

At this point in your life, you may have thousands of different habits. Some of these habits are good and healthy, and often contribute to you having a higher quality of life. Likewise, some of these habits are destructive and negative, and often take away from your quality of life. Knowing how to get your habits under control through your conscious effort and awareness will help you start to take responsibility for these habits, break the toxic ones, and develop a life that is more fulfilling and successful.

As you read through this book, you will quickly realize that despite how our brains work, we are not nearly as "out of control" with our habits as we tend to think we are. As well, you are not at the mercy of bad habits, and it is actually quite a bit easier to change habits or create new habits than you might think.

Rather than waiting for extraordinary events to occur in your life, such as winning the lottery or meeting your soulmate or magically landing the job of your dreams, get ready to take control of your life *right now*. Nothing and no one can have as big of an impact on your ability to take control over yourself and your actions as you can, which is exactly why you need to be ready to take responsibility for yourself and your success in life.

If you are ready to scrap the limiting belief that "habits are hard to break" or "bad habits die hard" and start learning how to ditch bad habits and formulate good ones quickly and effectively, you are in the right place. It's time for you to officially ditch the idea of chance and struggle and start knowing with absolute CERTAINTY that you have the ultimate power over your life. Let's begin!

Chapter 1

Your Habits Drive Your Lifestyle

"Whoever becomes a slave to habit, dies slowly" Martha Medeiros

People have an overwhelming tendency to blame their habits for why they are unable to create the results that they desire in life. Constantly, you hear of people saying things like "I would work out in the morning, but I can never wake up early enough" or "I would eat healthier, but it takes too much time to shop for and cook healthier recipes, plus I don't know how." What people are really saying is that they are in the habit of waking up late, or shopping for and eating convenience meal items and they do not know how to break this habit. Rather than accepting responsibility for it, they allow that habit to overrule their lives and prevent them from achieving their goals. What's more is that these individuals genuinely believe that they are incapable of making change because of how deeply rooted these habits are and how difficult it is for them to uproot these habits. This is because, for the most part, people are uneducated on what habits actually are, why they exist, and the real neuroscience behind how you can change a habit easily and for good.

Everyone Has Unconscious Habits

Everyone, regardless of who they are, has unconscious habits. Whether you are brand new to addressing your habits, or you have been addressing them for years, you have unconscious habits that exist in your life that affect you in one way or another. Unconscious habits are habits that you develop without realizing it or habits that you unintentionally created through repetitive behavior. These habits are developed right from a very young age in your life and continue to be created for as long as you are alive. Even when you are consciously creating your habits, you will still be creating unconscious habits along the way.

Most of your current unconscious habits come from engaging in repetitive behavior without fully realizing the effect that this has on your brain. Some of them may have been taught to you by your parents, such as to make your bed and brush your teeth when you wake up, while you may have learned others on your own, such as what direction to drive to work in the morning or when to check your emails or social media updates. Either way, every single one of these habits was developed through repetitive behavior that you either knowingly or unknowingly engaged in for a period of time.

While unconscious habits can continue to be developed even after you have more conscious control over your habits, they are most prominent and affect your life the most prior to you taking conscious control over your habits. This is especially true of habits that began in childhood or that are rooted in beliefs that began in childhood, as these habits and beliefs are based on what other people told you and were developed at a time when you could not consciously dispute them. The longer a habit is carried for, or the more deeply attached it is to a deeply-rooted belief of yours, the stronger that habit will be, and the more it will affect you. In fact, it may even become so strong and impactful that you do not realize it is a habit, or that you have any level of control over it. This is often why people behave like they are victims at the mercy of their habits because they do not know any better.

It is true that unconscious habits will always exist, but it does not mean that they have to run amok in your life. When you learn how to address and navigate your habits, you will discover that it is actually easier to source and eliminate a habit than you may currently believe. Through this fail-proof process, you will be able to identify, uproot, and eliminate as many problematic habits as possible. While it will take time, and it will require you to be patient, it is possible and in due time, you will find yourself consciously in control of at least the majority of your habits. For those which you may not consciously be in control over, you will still have the strength to mindfully navigate them so as to lessen their negative impact on your life.

Your Habits Drive Your Lifestyle

The habits you keep are largely responsible for the lifestyle you currently have. People who choose to keep habits that keep them stuck or engaging in behaviors that are counterintuitive to what it is that they truly want for themselves will continue to experience a reality that fails to give them the results they desire in their lives. This is incredibly common amongst people who are unaware of and, therefore, no consciously in control over their habits.

Even when you do become aware of your habits, however, you can start to find yourself experiencing trouble with actually changing them unless you know the real secrets behind *how* to change them. Thus, you can feel as though you are trapped in an unwanted lifestyle and truly unable to escape because try as you might, you cannot bring yourself to make the necessary changes. If you are coming up against this frustration yourself, I encourage you to take a moment of pause and to celebrate yourself for being here, reading this book, and doing everything you can to learn how to change your habits and create new ones. Your devotion *will* pay off!

Anytime you desire to make a change to your lifestyle, it is critical that you drive that change first in your beliefs, and then in your habits. By creating change on these deeper levels, you are able to adjust your lifestyle in a way that is actually sustainable. Most guides surrounding lifestyle will encourage you to make changes using willpower when in reality, willpower is only intended to be used in short bursts. Attempting to make entire life changes on willpower alone will result in constant relapses, as soon as your willpower runs out. You *must* go deeper than willpower and into your beliefs and habits if you are going to make any lasting change.

As soon as you start integrating changes on a deeper level, you will start seeing serious changes in your lifestyle. At this point, lifestyle changes will no longer seem unstable or easy to shake because you will have confidence and certainty in these changes. Through this, you will be able to reliably believe in your changes and embrace them in every way possible.

How Bad Habits Keep You In a Low Quality Life

Your subconscious brain does not have the capacity to decipher "good" from "bad" which is why it can be so easy to develop bad habits, especially when you are not consciously aware of the habits you are creating. This is why, until they take control, so many people find themselves with a variety of bad habits that are affecting their lives and shaping their lifestyles.

Some of these bad habits may seem small and may seem like they have minimal impact on the overall quality of an individual's life. For example, if you don't make your bed in the morning or if you wear your shoes through the house and track mud across the floors, this may not seem like such a big deal. On an individual level, it's true; these are not necessarily habits that you need to be overly concerned about. However, if you find that you are later frustrated because the messy bed makes you feel like your room is chaotic, or because you have to put in extra effort to clean the mud off your floors, suddenly these "small" bad habits have a large impact on your life.

The culmination of bad habits in your life can lead to you driving an entire lifestyle that feels as though you are constantly cleaning up after yourself, or making you pay the price in the future for things that you are doing in the present. While this may not seem like a big deal at times, experiencing this on an ongoing basis can create a lifestyle that ultimately does not align with how you want to feel, or what you genuinely want for yourself in life.

Aside from smaller bad habits which can accumulate and create nuisances in your life, even to the point of completely transforming your lifestyle, larger bad habits can do the same. In fact, larger bad habits tend to be the ones that initially trigger people to realize that they need help in navigating their habits in the first place. You might find yourself struggling with bad habits like smoking, eating low-quality food, skipping your workouts too frequently, or spending so much money that you barely have enough to pay your bills at the end of every month. These types of habits tend to be obvious and have large, unavoidable consequences that can leave you feeling frustrated and overwhelmed with yourself and the habits you keep. Until you change them, you will continue to live at their mercy, too.

Bad habits can hold people back in virtually every area of their lives and can lead to them living a life that is unfulfilling, unaligned, and out of integrity with their authentic self, and that can even create negative and toxic consequences in their lives. The more you feed into these habits, the longer these consequences will be faced and the more emotional, mental, and physical turmoil you will likely face as a result.

How Good Habits Will Transform Your Life

While bad habits have the capacity to drive you toward having an unfulfilling and unaligned lifestyle, good habits can help you create the life of your dreams. A few consciously created and well-placed habits can transform your eating habits, your exercise routine, your success with your career, and many other areas of your life.

Good habits are designed to keep you in deep alignment with your desires and your goals, allowing you to create the lifestyle you truly desire. Through them, you are able to work effectively with your brain and your nature in such a way that allows you to consciously co-create your life by design. Everything flows easily, and it feels effortless to create the lifestyle you desire when you are working alongside good habits.

Chances are, even if you have not already been working with your habits on a conscious level, you have begun to experience the benefits of positive habits. Remember, your subconscious mind does not recognize the difference between good and bad, which means that just like you have already developed bad habits, you have already developed good habits, too. While most people do not recognize or give attention to their good habits because they are not causing any discomfort or problems in their lives, it is always a good idea to do your best to draw awareness to these habits. Becoming aware of and celebrating your good habits is a great way to recognize that you are already capable of enjoying good habits and that it is easy for you to create good habits in your life. This way, as you begin to consciously create good habits, you realize it is already easy and possible for you.

Some of the good habits you may already have include eating several times a day, communicating with your loved ones, brushing your teeth twice a day, or showering on a regular basis. These habits and any habits that contribute to you having a higher quality of life and a greater level of success in your life can all be considered good, positive habits. The more you can embrace these habits and use them to your advantage, the better your life will be. Ultimately, your goal when creating conscious habits is to create as many positive habits as possible so that you can drive a positive, happy, and fulfilling lifestyle that allows you to effortlessly and inevitably reach all of your goals.

The Eight Areas Of Your Life To Improve

In your life, there are eight primary areas that you are going to want to pay attention to when it comes to what types of habits you have and how these habits are affecting your wellbeing. Understand that as you address these eight areas of your life, you are not going to want to dive in and change or create new habits for every single area of your life all at once. In fact, you may not even want to start deeply analyzing the habits of each area of your life all at once, especially if you tend to be particularly overwhelmed by such work. Instead, you want to become aware of the fact that all eight areas of your life exist and that habits are currently affecting and influencing each of these eight areas of your life. You also want to work on taking responsibility for those habits and these areas of your life so that you can begin to have greater control over the life you are creating for yourself.

The first area of your life that you will want to consider is your health. Your health is affected by many things in your life, ranging from how you eat and how you exercise to how you set boundaries for yourself and what types of thoughts you routinely think about.

The second area of your life to consider is your wealth. Your wealth includes your finances, your budget, and any habits you have surrounding money. Wealth also covers non-money related material wealth, such as your belongings, your home, and habits surrounding other resources you have access to in your life.

The third area of your life that you need to consider is your career. Your career includes any professional endeavors you are engaged in, ranging from your full time career to your side ventures. If you are not presently employed, anything you do to seek work or in place of work qualifies as your career.

The fourth area of your life to be considered is your relationships. Any habits you have revolving relationships with family members, friends, co-workers, acquaintances, and even strangers you meet on a daily basis are all housed under the topic of relationships. These habits will include things such as how you create, maintain, manage, and end relationships in your life.

The fifth area of your life to consider is your romantic relationship or your love life. Habits revolving around how you meet romantic interests, how you engage with them, and what types of patterns you uphold in your relationships fall under this category. Your habits here may directly affect your partner or potential partners, or they may be entirely intrapersonal, such as how you think about romantic interests or the role you take on in relationships.

The sixth area of your life that you need to consider is your relationship with yourself. This includes how you talk to yourself, how you think about yourself, what you think about yourself, and the way you treat yourself. Habits revolving around how you care for your body, mind, and emotions, as well as habits that revolve around how you spend your alone time and how you feel being by yourself.

The seventh area of your life to consider is your hobbies and interests. You will need to become aware of how your habits result in you approaching your hobbies, committing to your hobbies, creating time for your hobbies, and otherwise engaging in hobbies. Pay attention to your interests as well, even those that do not manifest as hobbies or long term interests, as they can tell you a great deal about your habits, too.

Lastly, the eighth area of your life to consider is your faith or spirituality. If you are religious, this will include any habits you have around your religion. If you are of non-denominational faith or lack faith in anything at all, your habits will matter here, too. You can identify your habits based on how you approach your faith and how you tend to invest time in or share your faith with others.

Chapter 2

Quit Relying On Chance and Take Responsibility

One of the many problems with existing inside of the victim mentality that often accompanies a person that is entrenched with unconscious habits is the idea that everything in life comes down to "luck." Rather than taking radical responsibility for their lives and making changes so that they can enjoy the lives they want, they choose to believe that they are "not lucky" or that chance has yet to fall on their side to give them their dream life. Often, these individuals can be found waiting on a lottery ticket, a soulmate, or a dream job to magically fall into their laps so that their lives can change. The reality is, you and you alone are responsible for the quality of life, and waiting on the chance to create your desired results for you is a sign of laziness and a sign that you have succumbed to the victim mentality of unconscious habits.

If you have found yourself saying these things at one point in the past, even if it was in the recent past, I encourage you not to develop shame or feelings of embarrassment around having believed that chance was your one shiny hope for a better life. Our society is presently structured in a way that largely promotes the idea of banking on chance and getting comfortable in a not so comfortable life. Arguably, the circumstances that lead to you feeling that way are not entirely your fault. What you do now that you realize this is completely absurd and untrue, however, is your responsibility.

Chance Is Not Worth Betting Your Life On

Your life will only ever happen once. There is no guarantee that you will get a do over, or that you will be able to make up for the things you did not take advantage of or act on in the past. New opportunities are arriving every day, but if you never take advantage of them, then what does it matter? If you are so busy waiting on the chance to drop you with an extraordinary experience that you ignore or deny those opportunities, then the only person responsible for your misfortune is *you*.

Your life is precious, your time is precious, your energy is precious, and everything about your existence on earth is precious. If you do not yet believe that to be absolutely true, then trust that as you begin to take responsibility for yourself and your life, this will change, and you will find yourself having an entirely new outlook on life. Regardless of whether you are there or not, though, you need to start acting like your life is the most important thing that you have in this world – because *it is*. Banking the entire quality of your life on chance is one of the worst gambles we can take. If you take this type of chance with your life, you are setting yourself up with the odds stacked wildly against you, and with no chance of redeeming yourself from the constant misfortune that comes with this untasteful bet. The only way to free yourself of this misfortune and to start experiencing the luck you wish to experience is to take responsibility for yourself, your life, and your actions and to start changing your lifestyle on your own terms.

As Oprah Winfrey says: "Luck is preparation meeting opportunity." Luck is not things magically falling into your lap without you going out and doing something to make said things happen. Even if you wanted to win the lottery, find your soul mate, or get that great job, you would have to go out and make it happen. You would have to buy the ticket, start taking dating seriously and put the work in to ensure that you were qualified for your dream job. *Nothing* in your life happens without you first doing something in order to make it happen.

When you start to realize that even the extraordinary events that you are waiting on require action on your behalf, it no longer seems so unreasonable for you to put in the work on situations that are far more likely to work in your favor. For example, putting the work in on changing your diet, exercising more, keeping your home cleaner, learning new skills that support your career, or communicating in a way that is more harmonious with the loved ones in your life. All of these, plus many other wonderful changes can be made by realizing where you ought to be investing your faith, hope, and energy in order to actually create the results you desire. This way, you can stop being a victim of bad habits and luck and start being the creator of your own destiny.

Extraordinary Events Don't Make Extraordinary People

Before we dive into how you can begin to take responsibility for yourself and your habits, I want to dig a little deeper into the reason behind why most people wait on extraordinary events to change their lives, and why this is a bad idea. The concept of waiting for something extraordinary to happen before you are willing to make a life change is both lazy and absurd. In regards to laziness, this choice to wait on something special to happen gives you a great opportunity to justify why you are not taking action in your life and, therefore, why you do not see any results. It is a great copout for anyone who is afraid of the work or energy that it might take for them to see the results they desire, or for anyone who is afraid of failure or obsessed with perfectionism. As long as you always hold onto this concept of waiting on something special, you can continue to argue that it is "not your fault" that nothing has changed in your life. Of course, this is not true, but it can be easy to justify your lack of change in this way, and therefore many people cling to it.

In regards to absurdity, it is important that you realize that extraordinary events do not make for extraordinary people. For example, winning the lottery will not suddenly improve your life or give you everything you ever wanted. Likewise, finding your soulmate will not magically heal your romantic woes, and landing your dream job will not suddenly inspire you to start taking your work more seriously. Contrary to popular belief, these types of events do not inspire true change in anyone and, the change that is experienced will rapidly be lost when the novelty of this new change wears off, and the person realizes that they themselves never actually changed. As a result, you will quickly realize that these perceived fortunes were never the reason why you had not yet managed to change your life.

The real reason is that you decided not to engage in change is because you did not want to, or you were unwilling to learn how.

The only way that you can experience true change in your life is if you put the work in to make change happen. You have to be willing to become aware of what it takes to make change happen, and you have to be willing to put the work in to actually create this change so that the change can be long lasting. If you are unwilling to become aware of the process or put the work in, you are going to find yourself constantly experiencing more of the same old same old, because you yourself have chosen that. As far as the effort required to make changes, that is up to you. You get to decide how easy or how hard it will be for you to engage in change based on how much effort you are willing to put into finding a solution that works for you, and how committed you are to believing in that solution and seeing it through.

Taking Responsibility For the Quality Of Your Life

Now that you understand why waiting on extraordinary events for your life to change is absurd, you can start to take true responsibility for yourself. First, you need to start by taking responsibility for the quality of your life. Right now, all of the experiences that you are having in your health, wealth, career, relationships, love life, relationship with yourself, hobbies, and faith are all because of choices you have made. You, and you alone, are responsible for the quality of life that you are experiencing.

When I say this, understand that I am not trying to blame you for things beyond your control. Chronic illness, economic crashes, and certain hardships, for example, are not all your fault. Often, our lives are affected by external things that we truly cannot stop or change, and there is no way that we could even begin to. What I am saying, however, is that it is your choice whether or not you do the most within your capacity to ensure that you live the best life possible. For example, if you have a chronic illness, you are the one deciding whether or not to take your medicine or engage in habits that are going to support you in improving the quality of your life, no one else. Or, if you are experiencing poverty due to the economy, you are the one deciding whether or not to do something about it so that you can find new opportunities or at least offset the amount of hardship you are facing. No one can force you to talk to someone, take your medicine, look for new jobs, develop new skills, or try out new opportunities if you are unwilling to take action yourself. Furthermore, no one *will*. Even if you happen to be someone who has people in your corner pushing you to do better if you continually choose not to then eventually those people will give up and let you go about creating more of your own misfortune. Everyone has their limits.

Rather than blaming your family for how

they raised you, or your friends for how they treated you, or your education for how it failed you, or your job for laying you off, or whatever else you can think to blame, start taking responsibility. Realize that within your realm of opportunities in every situation lie two things: your judgment, and your voluntary actions. This means that you get to decide whether you are going to view something as a misfortune or a lesson, and you get to decide how you are going to navigate the cards you have been dealt. Many people navigate challenging situations in such a way that enables them to create seemingly miraculous circumstances, all because they believed it was possible, and they created the necessary habits to make it happen. Many others, however, navigate challenging situations in such a way that creates more challenges because they believe they are unlucky and that they are a victim of misfortune. As a result, they often also develop negative beliefs and habits that continue to draw them further away from the life they desire.

Taking Responsibility For the Habits You Have Created

In addition to taking responsibility for the quality of life you are presently experiencing, you also need to take responsibility for the habits that you have created. Now, this may seem challenging as some of those habits may be rooted from your youth or connected to beliefs you created as a young child. You may also want to argue that since you had no idea how habits were created, you could not possibly have stopped any unwanted habits from taking root. While all of this can be true, again, it is up to you to choose to take responsibility starting right now. You may not always be the one "at fault" for why things happened, but you can certainly take responsibility for the outcome and start taking action to improve your outcome.

As far as your habits go, realize that in taking personal responsibility for every single habit you have created, you also take back your personal power, which supports you in undoing every single unwanted habit and creating new, healthier habits. When you are the one in control, you get to decide what happens. Until you are truly taking responsibility for where you are at in life, you will only be using your control to place that control outside of yourself where it is not useful.

You need to decide as of right now that every habit you have created is your responsibility. Finding out where that habit came from, why it exists, and what drives it is your responsibility. It is your responsibility to understand how to shift that habit or replace that habit, or how to ensure that you are engaging in said habit consciously and with intention. You are responsible for any circumstances that habit produces, and for the results of your own actions. Even if it feels like you cannot help yourself or it seems impossible to stop engaging in said habit, it is your responsibility.

The more you can take radical responsibility for your habits, the easier it will be for you to start making serious changes to your habits so that you can begin shifting them. The best way to start taking radical responsibility is to say, "I am responsible for this" every single time you witness yourself engaging in a habit, and during every step of the way. For example, when you realize a habit has been triggered, say, "I am responsible for this." When you carry out that habit, say, "I am responsible for this." When you experience the aftermath of engaging in your habit, say, "I am responsible for this." This way, you can start getting into the mindset of taking back your power and you can set yourself up to start truly making changes in your life.

Identifying Damaging Habits You Have Been Holding Onto

As you begin to take responsibility for your quality of life and habits, it may feel particularly challenging to identify and take responsibility for damaging habits. After all, damaging habits have been creating chaos in your life, and taking responsibility means that you realize that in the past, you contributed to that chaos and that in the future, you are responsible for any chaos that is created, too. Most of us do not want to admit that we are responsible for our own suffering, which can make it easy to reject the idea of damaging habits being our responsibility. In the end, though, this only hurts you and worsens your suffering.

For now, let's lean into the process of working with your habits in a way that promotes you taking radical responsibility for the habits you are carrying. You are going to do this by identifying at least one damaging habit that you have been holding onto, uncovering the entire habit itself to the best of your ability, and taking responsibility for that habit. Once you have done this for one habit, you will want to start doing it for every single habit you have, destructive or not.

You can start to identify your damaging habits by looking for symptoms of destruction in your life. Look at areas of your life where you experience hardship, toxic patterns, or drama on a regular basis. This may be in your relationships, in your health practices, or anywhere else in your life, where you find yourself continually struggling to enjoy a positive and healthy experience. Once you have located an area of your life with said symptoms, write it down and write down all of the symptoms you have noticed. Then, start looking at all of the actions you take around these symptoms that either contribute to them, cause them, or come after the symptoms have been experienced. You will likely begin to notice a pattern of how you tend to behave and contribute to said situations that will allow you to begin to witness your own role in them. Now, you need to take responsibility for this pattern. You need to accept that, in one way or another, you have agreed to continue acting on this pattern, and that you have been responsible for this pattern continuing. In taking responsibility for it, you also need to take responsibility for the outcome this habit has had on your life, and for the way it has affected your overall quality of life.

It may take you a little while to accept full responsibility for your role in a certain habit, but as long as you continue working toward owning it, you will find yourself taking full responsibility for it. Then, you will have accepted full power over your ability to shift it so that you are no longer being affected by this pattern anymore. We will talk more about how to do this in *Chapter 10: How To Break Bad Habits*.

Chapter 3

The Facts About Habits

Now that we have done some work around your mindset surrounding your habits let's dig into some cold hard facts surrounding what habits are, where they are formed in the brain, how they form, and why habits exist in the first place. This fact-based approach to dealing with habits helps you understand the neuroscience behind a habit which, in many ways, will give you a deeper sense of awareness around why habits are so important to your wellbeing. This will also support you in understanding what is going on when habits are being developed, or removed, which can remove a great deal of the mystery around habits themselves. This way, rather than wondering why breaking bad habits can be so hard, and why willpower alone is not enough when it comes to breaking bad habits or starting good ones, you can have the exact answers you need to navigate your habits effectively.

Note that the neuroscience and facts in this book are as up-to-date as possible at the time of writing this, but science is constantly evolving, and there is always more to be learned. For that reason, it is always a good idea to keep an eye out for the latest research studies done on habits so that you can further improve your understanding of how habits work and how you can leverage habits to your benefit. Even if you think you have the process down pat, refining it even just a little more at a time can make it easier and easier for you to reach your goals and truly embrace the life you want to live.

What Is a Habit?

One great quote that can help you understand the power of habits and the importance of habits was by Mahatma Gandhi. In it, he said, "Your beliefs become your thoughts, your thoughts become your words, your words become your actions, your actions become your habits, your habits become your values, and your values become your destiny." This quote truly outlines the power that habits have in our lives, as well as the general outline for how they are designed and how they affect us, and our long term wellbeing.

It is no secret that habits are powerful and that they are influenced by you, but what *are* habits exactly? The most direct description of a habit is "a behavior pattern acquired by frequent repetition or physiologic exposure that shows itself in regularity or increased facility of performance," which can be found in the Meriam-Webster Dictionary. Ultimately, habits are a series of behaviors that you engage in on a regular basis, in the exact same way every time, for the same reason, and with the same immediate benefit.

There is often some misconception around what constitutes as a habit, and what does not. Some researchers like to view habits on a spectrum that shows a different range of "dedication" to a habit that you may have. On one end of the spectrum, you have a behavioral pattern that has not yet become routine, meaning that it is a chosen behavioral pattern that you have to consciously choose to engage in and that may change from time to time. On the other end of the spectrum, you have a full blown addiction that is so deeply ingrained in your brain and life that you repeat it at the same time, the same way, without fail, and if you do not, you experience serious repercussions for skipping the habit. For example, people who have a habit of smoking will often experience migraines, anger, and tell-tale symptoms of withdrawal if they skip a cigarette break.

Certain habits are reinforced by behavior and natural chemical reactions within the brain alone. These habits are ones where no substance is introduced to the body, and therefore there is no alteration of consciousness or state of being when the habit is engaged in, beyond what the body naturally produces itself. Other habits are reinforced by behavioral and natural chemical reactions within the brain, as well as by addictive substances that can magnify the natural habit-creation process. These types of habits are far more likely to become addicting because of the added substances that cause the habit to "hook" much deeper into the brain and to have much more significant consequences if it is not engaged.

For the purpose of this book, we are talking about habits that are non-substance related, although those that are substance-related can still be benefited by the material within this book. However, anyone can benefit from this information and can use it toward breaking habits. I only ask that you ensure that you have the proper support and medical care if you are working through habits that involve addictive substances to avoid dealing with any negative medical repercussions by following this process.

Where Are Habits Formed In the Brain?

Deep in the cerebral hemispheres of your brain, there is a group of structures known as the basal ganglia. These structures include the putamen, the caudate, and the globus pallidus in the cerebrum. They also include the subthalamic nucleus in the diencephalon and the substantia nigra in the midbrain. The basal ganglia has a strong connection with the cerebral cortex, the brainstem, the thalamus, and other parts of your brain and are therefore involved in many different functions of the brain. Some of these functions include voluntary motor movements, habit learning, procedural learning, cognition, eye movement, and emotion.

As far as habit learning goes, the basal ganglia works by identifying a system of routines that can be repeated based on a specific trigger, and that produces a specific emotional reward. Upon identifying this system of routines, it begins to recognize it, learn it, and integrate it as a habit into your brain. Some of the more practical habits that your basal ganglia has helped you learn include exercising, parallel parking, brushing your teeth, and driving your typical route to work. That's not all, though. Every single habit you have *ever* made was formed within the basal ganglia.

Once a habit is identified, the basal ganglia works to memorize it perfectly, almost like a machine-learning computer learning a piece of code. As soon as the "code" is memorized enough, your brain integrates it as a habit. This process effectively removes the conscious thinking and decision making patterns from that particular behavior so that you no longer have to consciously think about how to do something, or make decisions around it. Instead, your brain already knows what to do and what decisions to make, and it does so automatically. As a result, the habit is formed and executed.

The process of your conscious thinking and decision making patterns being removed from the habit is largely what makes navigating the process of changing or breaking habits so challenging. At this point, a habit is truly wired into your brain, and it will take a lot more than some willpower and elbow grease to get it out of there. Now, you need to understand how the "coding" of your brain works so that you can essentially change the code within your brain. This may sound easy, but when you realize that all of these pieces of code coincide with each other and that one single habit affects so many areas of your life, as well as so many other habits, you begin to see how changing or breaking a habit can become so difficult. At this point, you are not just changing one thing; you are changing multiple things. For this reason, the most effective approach is the one that has the least disruption to the existing code, yet has enough of a disruption to be able to eliminate the unwanted habit itself.

How Long Does It Take To Form a Habit?

There is a lot of mixed information on how long it actually takes to form a habit. At one point, it was popularized that it only takes 21 days for a habit to form, but the truth is that after 21 days, the habit is still in its infancy. At this point, you have begun to develop a strong habit but it would still be incredibly easy for you to break or disrupt this new habit. As soon as it was broken, it would be easy to abandon the habit and would take a great deal of effort to reintegrate it. While it would not be quite so hard because you had put effort into learning it in the first place, and therefore neural pathways had been formed, it would still be very challenging.

Recent science has shown that it takes an average of 66 days for a habit of becoming automatic, although there are a lot of variables that can affect the validity of this. For example, an individual's behavior, beliefs, personality, and circumstances can all impact how quickly they are able to integrate a new habit and maintain that habit as a true automatic behavior. Because of these variables, it is generally agreed upon that it can take anywhere from 18 to 254 days for a new habit to be properly formed. Once a person has reached the 254 day mark of repeating the behavioral pattern of the new habit, regardless of where they fall in the range of variables, there is a very strong chance that they have embraced a true habit, making the behavior automatic.

What Is the Benefit Of Habits?

Despite the fact that bad habits can lead to unwanted results and hardships in your life, habits themselves actually have a very important and beneficial role in your life. Habits themselves are used to help you engage in life in a way that results in your brain using less energy, leaving you with a greater ability to divert your conscious awareness toward something else. For example, when you go to the bathroom, you do not have to think about how to sit down, how to go to the bathroom, how to wipe, how to flush, and how to wash your hands. Instead, all of this is a habit and you likely do it in the same way (or close to) every single time. As you are doing this, you may be thinking about what you need to do after you have finished going to the bathroom, or daydreaming about something new that you want to try.

Practical habits exist in all areas of your life as a way to make important and necessary behaviors easier while also reducing the amount of energy they require. From a neuroscientific point of view, if a behavior is automatic, then it requires less of your brain function in order for that behavior to be executed. This way, you save energy. Believe it or not, your body uses up the majority of your daily calories when you are resting, *not* when you are actually exercising, which means reducing your energy usage during rest is still vitally important for your body.

In addition to habits helping you through practical things in life, they can also help you through mastery, or through progressive development. For example, let's say you are an artist, and your chosen medium is drawing. If you had not developed habits on how to hold your pencil, how to draw basic lines and shapes, and how to engage in other seemingly basic drawing skills, it would be virtually impossible to master the art of drawing. You would have to relearn the basic behaviors over and over again, thus preventing you from being able to build on them by developing habits that are more aligned with mastery levels of drawing.

Habits also help you when it comes to consciously choosing your lifestyle and achieving your goals through various points in your life. If you develop good habits, you can help yourself achieve certain goals and outcomes effortlessly because you do not have to consciously think about taking the actions that will get you the results. Instead, your brain *automatically* engages in these actions, thus making it virtually effortless for you to create the success you desire. In many ways, your success is inevitable because you have wired your brain to make it happen.

Can We Live Without Habits?

Given the nature of habits, it is impossible to completely rid your life of habits. Furthermore, you would not want to. While some people may claim to live habit-free, what they are generally talking about is being free from bad habits, or from habits that are non-essential to standard everyday life. For example, they may live free of habits surrounding TV usage, reading, engaging in hobbies, and performing other non-essential behaviors. However, they will still have habits that support them in driving, cooking, using the washroom, cleaning themselves, and otherwise taking care of their livelihood. While they may be bringing conscious awareness to these habits through mindfulness, they are not breaking the habits or defying the habits per se. Instead, they are simply becoming aware of the habits, their benefits, and the steps involved in completing those habits.

Instead of trying to rid yourself of all habits, you can focus on eliminating and shifting habits that are giving you negative results, or that are not giving you the results you truly desire. This way, you are no longer carrying ineffective habits that are going to create unwanted outcomes in your life. You can also eliminate any non-essential habits that are not bringing you positive results, even if they are not bringing you negative results, either. In doing so, you create the capacity for you to develop habits that will be far more effective, and that will bring you far greater benefits in your life.

As you work to shift your habits, you can also work toward increasing your mindfulness so that while you are engaging in habits, you are able to bring your conscious awareness to them. This way, you are able to be mindful of each step in the habit and you can take inventory on how helpful the habit is, or whether or not it is truly worth it for you to engage in the said habit. You can also use this mindful awareness to decide whether you want to keep engaging in the habit, shift it, or change it altogether. Working alongside your habits in this more mindful manner is far more productive than attempting to truly live habit-free, as doing so would require a significant amount of conscious awareness and energy and, ultimately, would not be ideal.

Chapter 4

Three Step Habit Loops

As your basal ganglia works toward identifying behavioral patterns that can be developed into habits, it works through what is called a three step habit loop. This three step process can be broken down into a few sub steps. However, each of these three primary steps must be completed in order for a habit loop to be developed. Once a habit loop is developed your brain recognizes it and keeps it in its awareness so that it can spot any repetitions of this habit loop that you may be engaging in. The more times you repeat your habit loop, the more times you will reinforce said habit and the stronger it will become. Eventually, you have reinforced it so many times that the necessary neural pathways have been developed, strengthened, and put on autopilot.

Having a clear understanding of what this three step habit loop is, what it entails, and what sub steps are included in the habit loop helps you begin to identify how you can develop your own habits by working with your brain instead of against it. This is the first major step toward creating habits that will be effortless to maintain, sustainable, and effective toward helping you develop the lifestyle you desire.

The Three Steps Of a Habit Loop

The three steps of a habit loop are as follows: a cue, a routine, and a reward. Your basal ganglia will work together to identify these three steps through your everyday behaviors, whether you are consciously aware of it or not. Essentially, anytime you engage in a pattern, your brain, through your basal ganglia, will spot the three steps of that pattern including the cue, the routine, and the reward. Patterns with a larger reward will be more prominently memorized, whereas those with a smaller reward may not be memorized until they have been repeated a few times over.

After the initial memorization of a pattern, your brain will be looking for that pattern and will recognize anytime it has been repeated. It will then measure the number of repetitions to the size of the reward to determine the benefit of that habit and, the better the reward, the more likely it will be for you to continue engaging in that habit. This is how all habits are designed, whether they are designed consciously or unconsciously.

To consciously design a habit, your goal is not to change the habit loop, but instead to identify what it is and to consciously create a cue, routine, and reward that is worthy enough of your brain memorizing it and integrating it as a habit. As long as you continue to consciously engage in this habit, your brain will continue to reinforce it until, eventually, it becomes automatic. From there, you will no longer have to exert as much conscious thought or decision making into the process because it will happen all on its own.

Step One: The Cue

The cue of a habit is often the most elusive part of unconsciously designed habits because it is a random trigger that your brain has identified and associated with your habit in question. In some cases, the cue may become obvious, whereas, in others, it could remain a mystery for some time until you do some sleuthing to identify what the cue actually is.

A cue is any trigger that will encourage your brain to start engaging in a habitual process. For example, when you wake up, you may find yourself immediately going to the bathroom, and then going to the kitchen to make a coffee. The cue here is waking up, while the routine is going to the bathroom and then making your coffee.

Unconscious cues can be associated with anything that can affect your five senses, which is why they can be so challenging to uncover. A smell, sight, sound, touch, or taste could all trigger the response of a habit loop. Cues can also be associated with specific behaviors or with other habits, thus adding to the complexity of cues. For example, you may be in the habit of eating dinner and then immediately having a dessert after your dinner. In this case, the habit of eating dessert is directly associated with the habit of eating dinner. If you eat dinner at a certain time, then that time would trigger the habit. If you have dinner immediately after getting home from work, yet you get home from work at different times of the day, then getting home from work would be the trigger for dinner.

As you can see, cues can be rather complex and can be associated with just about anything. The best way to identify the trigger of an existing habit is to begin to pay attention to exactly what you are doing the moment you begin to engage in said habit, as well as exactly what you were doing in the moments before you engaged in that habit. Be sure to explore all five of your senses, as well as your circumstances, to ensure that you have a full understanding around what it is that is the cue for your habit.

When you begin to consciously create habits, you are going to want to intentionally develop your cue. Through this, you can decide what specifically will result in you engaging in your habit. Then, you will go ahead and consciously interact with your cue immediately before following through on the routine so that your brain makes the association. At this point, the unconscious work going on in your basal ganglia will be exactly the same; the only difference is that you will be directing it with your conscious mind.

Step Two: The Routine

The routine of your habit is the part where you engage in the habit itself. This isolated part of the habit routine is often seen as the habit in its entirety by people who are unclear on what a three step habit loop actually is, or who are unclear on how the brain works when it is developing habits.

The routine of your habit is the behavioral pattern that your basal ganglia is looking out for so that it can keep track of the actions you are taking that are associated with the developing or developed habit. Here, your basal ganglia wants repetition that happens in the exact same way every single time. This means that you are going to complete each step of the routine in the same way, in the same order, every single time you engage in your habit loop.

For unconscious habits, your basal ganglia may start by getting a general idea of what it is that you are doing, and in what order you are doing it. Over time, it will start to help you "refine" these steps until they have been designed in such a way that it is easy to repeat in the same way, in the same order, every single time. At this point, each step is as much a habit as each overall routine is. The basal ganglia knows the routine is over when your brain experiences a reward. This reward is typically a chemical reaction in the brain that produces a positive feeling, thus making habits addicting and easy for you to repeat.

When you are looking to consciously develop new habits in your life, you want to identify a set routine that you can do in the same way, in the same order, every single time you consciously engage in your routine. For added benefit, you should be consciously thinking about each step that you are engaging in and the order you are engaging in it through so that you can draw your direct attention and awareness to this information. This way, your subconscious mind is more likely to absorb that information in its intended order and, through that, create your desired habit.

It is very important that you do exactly the same thing in exactly the same way to the best of your ability every single time. You must also consciously engage in your cue *before* the routine so that your brain begins to associate the routine with the said cue. This is how you can start to form a real habit loop in your brain that will become automatic and effortless. If it is easier for you to remember, consider your cue as "step one" of your habit every single time, and in every single habit you create.

Step Three: The Reward

The reward is perhaps the most important part of the entire habit loop. Within the reward, your brain determines whether a habit is worthy enough of its attention, and whether or not it deserves to be turned into a habit. The better the reward, the more likely a habit will be developed, and the stronger that habit will become.

In your brain, there is a portion known as the "reward system," which is responsible for what is known as "incentive salience." Incentive salience refers to motivation and wanting desire and craving for a specific reward. Whenever you engage in a habit, your brain produces a rewarding effect and, then, begins to crave that rewarding effect which encourages you to engage in the behavior again and again. Rewards are generally experienced in emotions such as joy, euphoria, or ecstasy. During the process of a reward, your brain produces dopamine which is responsible for developing those positive and oftentimes addictive emotional experiences.

There are three types of rewards you will experience when you engage in a habit, primary rewards, intrinsic rewards, and extrinsic rewards. Primary rewards are ones that facilitate the survival of one's self and offspring, which can include eating, engaging in sexual contact with your partner, and raising your child. Intrinsic rewards are considered to be unconditioned and create a deep sense of inner and personal pleasure whenever they are fulfilled. Extrinsic rewards are those which are conditioned and are attractive but are not inherently pleasurable and include things like making money or watching your favorite sports team win a game.

Through the reward center in your brain, you learn to engage more positive behaviors and refrain from engaging in harmful behaviors. From a primal point of view, this helps entire species continue to thrive by allowing them to engage in behaviors that positively affect their survival and wellbeing and avoiding behaviors that could cause damage or kill them off. Of course, it is not perfect, and many species, humans and non-humans alike, will engage in behaviors that can have harmful side effects because they are capable of producing a reward-like experience in the brain. For example, eating junk foods or consuming harmful substances that are able to support your reward system in producing addictive rewards.

The Anatomy Of a Strong Reward

As you begin to take responsibility for your own habits, you will find that you need to learn how to effectively navigate the reward center of your brain in order to cement habits in. Rewards are the entire motivator behind habits, and, arguably, they are as uniquely complex as the entire habit loop itself. Knowing how to pick positive rewards as a way to reward yourself for engaging in your chosen habit is important, as it will allow you to trigger an actual chemical reaction in your brain that rewards you for your experience, and motivates you to do it again.

Primal rewards are unlikely to be relevant or even remotely helpful in most of the habits that you are going to want to create for yourself. Extrinsic rewards, while enjoyable, are often not nearly as motivating as intrinsic rewards, meaning that while they are important, they are unlikely to provide you with the motivation that you need. As well, you may not have the resources to provide yourself with extrinsic rewards every time you engage in a new habit, which means this form of reward may be unrealistic for you. Intrinsic rewards, then, are the last route and are the best way for you to go.

Intrinsic rewards are any rewards that provide you personally with a deepened sense of joy and fulfillment. They can be elicited by external events, but they rarely give you a lasting, tangible reward. Instead, they give you a deep inner feeling of joy, euphoria, or ecstasy that allow you to feel incredibly positive for the activities that you have engaged in. Thus, your goal when creating a positive reward for your habit loop is to identify rewards that are going to give you unlimited intrinsic reward.

The key to picking an intrinsic reward that is going to rapidly and effectively cement your new habits into place is to choose one that is going to make you feel incredibly good, and one that can be completed immediately after engaging in the new habit. This way, your basal ganglia immediately recognizes the cue, routine, and reward, and your reward center is able to be abundantly boosted in order to create the results you desire.

Some ideal rewards you could use to reinforce your new habits include: calling a loved one and having a positive and enjoyable phone call, having a few minutes of you-time where you give yourself unconditional attention and care, a pep talk to yourself in the mirror, a happy dance as soon as you complete the new habit, or a moment for deeply felt and expressed gratitude. These are all rewards that can be engaged in quickly that are not contingent upon resources, and that will provide an abundance of joy, euphoria, or ecstasy in your brain so that your habit loop is complete and strong enough to motivate you to complete it again.

Chapter 5

Diverting Your Desire

While habits are often seen as a repeated routine of behaviors by your conscious mind, the real driving force behind habits is the reward cycle for your subconscious mind. For that reason, knowing how to work with your desire in a proper and healthy manner is far more conductive than attempting to work against your desire in order to change your habits. This is a key factor that many people miss because they do not realize how truly powerful and necessary the reward and desire is for their ability to effectively create, shift, and break habits.

To put it in layman's terms, your brain creates micro-addictions to things that are enjoyable for you so that you will do more of them. It also creates aversions to things that are not enjoyable so that you will do less of them, exactly as you learned when we discussed rewards. In order to effectively develop new habits, then you need to be able to identify how to create the same form of desire through a new system of actions. If you fail to complete this process, any habit you are attempting to form will be driven solely on willpower which will inevitably run out and result in you no longer following through on this new habit. For many people, this pattern will also create a feeling of shame within you as you continually fail to achieve your desired result and have to face the embarrassment of admitting defeat on yet another goal. As this shame cycle grows, it becomes harder and harder to embrace new habits because your willpower dwindles *and* you grow to stop believing in yourself and your ability to engage in new habits.

Fortunately, shifting your approach to include a redirection of your desire rather than attempting to deny your desire is all you need to correct this experience. This way, you can begin to experience new habits, achieve your desired goals, and break the cycle of shame as you realize that the problem was not with you but with your approach to the habit-forming cycle.

Resisting Desire Creates Relapses

Let's explore what the average approach to changing a habit looks like before an individual is educated on how to effectively work with the nature of their brain to facilitate change. Say you decide you want to change your diet so that you can reach your ideal weight and stamina, so you go to the bookstore and find a book that discusses a diet that can help you reach your needs. You educate yourself on this book, you get excited about the recipes and the extrinsic reward, and you are thrilled to get started. Amidst all your excitement, you toss out all of the food in your kitchen that does not fit the diet and you immediately begin eating this new way. For the first few days, or maybe even the first couple of weeks, everything is going great. You are pushing through cravings, you are eating every meal, and you are reaching all of your targets that you have set out for yourself. Things are *awesome*.

And then suddenly the momentum drops. You stop feeling so excited about the diet, and your cravings start feeling a little stronger. The novelty of this new diet has worn off; maybe you have seen some of the rewards for your change but not all of the rewards you had hoped for or it feels as though they are taking far too long to arrive. You think "just this once I'll eat something that does not adhere to my diet" and you cave. And suddenly, you can't stop. You held out on fulfilling that desire for so long that now, not only are you eating what you shouldn't be, but you are eating way more and you can't seem to reel yourself in. Your relapse, as we will call it, may even be worse than your original habit because the abstinence of desire made the fulfillment of desire *so* much better. And thus, your diet is broken and you are back where you started, if not worse.

Anytime you resist desire, you are setting yourself up for failure. Your brain is not wired to resist desire, and there is no good reason for you to attempt to resist desire, either. You can work within the realm of observing, being mindful of, and even delaying desire to a degree, but attempting to resist it indefinitely will create incredibly negative feelings around your new habit, which will eventually lead to you ditching the habit altogether. It may seem like you did so because you were lazy or not strong enough to keep going, but the opposite is actually true. You were incredibly strong to go as long as you did, because you were literally denying your brain of the thing it was craving, meaning that you denied your very nature. This requires magnificent strength and required you to use your willpower alone to push through for as long as you did. Eventually, though, that strength ran out and as soon as it did the new behavior fell apart.

Whenever this happens, you can feel confident that what you were creating was *not* a new habit. In order for it to have been a new habit, you would have needed to fulfill the craving for desire by engaging in a positive reward. Instead, you were engaging in a chosen repeated behavior that was running entirely through your conscious mind, thus defying the very point of a habit, which is to sink a chosen behavior into your subconscious mind so that it becomes automatic.

The only way to stop engaging in this battle of willpower and to prevent yourself from experiencing yo-yo like behavior as you bounce back and forth with new "habits" is to introduce desire back into the mixture. The key is to introduce desire intentionally, mindfully, and in such a way that promotes your desired outcome so that you are far more likely to actually reach it. When you can do this, then you will create true habits that are easy to build, easy to maintain, and that are far more likely to actually sink into your subconscious mind with the support of your basal ganglia and your reward system.

While creating a new habit in this manner will reduce the instance of relapses, it is important to note that it will not prevent them altogether. Once a habit loop has been established in the brain, it is extremely easy for that habit to be reengaged at any point in the future. While it does become less and less likely for it to be engaged, it can be, and thus, you must always be mindful of your behavior to ensure that you are never slipping into an old habit loop again. Remember, habit loops are triggered by a complex system of cues and, for that reason, it can sometimes be hard to ensure that you effectively rewire your behavior around every single cue associated with any given habit. The most effective way to navigate these potential relapses is to be mindful of your behavior, to witness anytime you see yourself slipping into old habits, and to use willpower to help you shift back into your preferred habit. Then, rely on the cycle of cue, routine, and reward (desire) to allow you to carry on with that new habit. Through this, you will be effectively balancing mindfulness, willpower, and desire to create strong, lasting habits that support you in reaching your goals in life.

Identifying Your True Desire

Much like how cues can be rather elusive at times, identifying your true desire can be elusive at times, too. With rewards existing in three forms, primal, intrinsic, and extrinsic, we can summarize that there are also three forms of desire: the desire to fulfill primary rewards, the desire to fulfill intrinsic rewards, and the desire to fulfill extrinsic rewards. Generally speaking, when it comes to developing new habits, the best approach is to focus largely on intrinsic desire while also recognizing extrinsic desire. This way, you are focusing on the most deeply fulfilling desire and reward system that is within your control, as well as an additional desire and reward system that has a positive impact on your life and your capacity to reach your worldly goals.

If you have been living your life with unconscious habits, you may not clearly understand what your desires are or what actually motivates you to engage in new habits. It may also feel challenging for you to identify each specific desire attached to each specific habit so that you can effectively navigate the redirection of that particular desire. As with discovering cues, some sleuthing can be helpful as it will support you in discovering what your actual desires are and how you can use those desires to create strong and positive habits.

One way you can begin to identify desire and the specific reward being gained from a habit you are engaging in is to identify what you are thinking about during the fulfillment of that habit and what you are most fulfilled by immediately after it. See if you can keep a log of each time you engage in that habit for the next few days or weeks, depending on how frequently you engage in said habit and keep track of this information. You should begin to see a pattern in desire or motivation and rewards being gained from your habit relatively quickly, allowing you to realize what it is that you are looking for and gaining every single time you engage in this behavior.

Another way to dig into what your desires are is to start paying attention to your emotions. Through your emotions, you can start to identify your general desires, which will allow you to gain a stronger understanding of what drives you in general. This way, you can begin to use this to understand what is likely to be driving you in each individual habit, thus narrowing down that which may be affecting you and supporting you with shifting your habits more quickly.

Jealousy is a very important emotion to watch for when it comes to desire, as you will often experience jealousy around people who have something that you want. You may be jealous of a specific person, or of something in particular that many people may have in common. For example, you may be jealous of your friend, or you may be jealous anytime you see someone in a positive, healthy romantic relationship. When you witness yourself experiencing jealousy, start asking yourself questions to identify why you are jealous, or what it is that you wish you had that someone else has. Anytime you feel jealous, it is because you desire something that someone else has, which can help you uncover a desire that you are experiencing that seems as though it is going unfulfilled.

You should also pay attention anytime you feel uncomfortable or anytime you experience a "no way" response; for example, "there's no way I could do that!" Discomfort shows you anytime there is something in your life that you do not want, which allows you to then examine what it is that you do want. For example, maybe anytime you talk to a certain person you experience discomfort so you try to push through it or avoid that person in order to avoid the discomfort. Upon further examination, you may realize that the reason why that discomfort exists is that this person tends to cross your boundaries when you are talking to them, which means that you desire for more boundaries. The "no way" response is a specific form of discomfort that means that you feel a level of intimidation and admiration from something that you are being faced with. If you were truly disinterested in something, your response would be less emotionally charged because you would not care about the experience or event. When you experience this emotional response to something that makes you uncomfortable through intimidation and admiration, this means that there is likely an unexpressed or unexplored desire hidden in there that you need to explore.

It is also important to realize that after you have had a particular habit for any given period of time, it may begin to develop new rewards unto itself that continue to reinforce that particular habit.

One big reward in particular that tends to be experienced by people who engage in long time habits is the reward of familiarity. Familiarity keeps us comfortable by keeping our surroundings and our lives familiar and predictable, which means that we can switch off of surveillance mode and relax from time to time. In these settings, your primal brain knows that you are unlikely to be at risk of experiencing any incoming threats, so you can simply relax and be at ease in your life. Be aware of these secondary rewards when you are looking through existing habits to ensure that you are truly seeing the entirety of what you are gaining from each habit you explore. This way, you know exactly what needs to happen in order for you to fully shift away from that habit.

As you begin to identify these general desires that you have, you can use them to help you develop new habits, or to change existing habits that you already have. This is an excellent way to step out of the practice of denying your desire and into the practice of leveraging your desire to create positive habits.

Redirecting Your True Desire

Once you uncover your true desire, you need to start identifying ways that you can redirect your desire. This is going to be a two-step process: first, you are going to identify what the desire is and how it could be fulfilled in different, healthier ways. Then, you are going to define a specific routine that is going to help you achieve the fulfillment of that desire, and it's reward in a way that is far more positive and healthy for you.

Understand that true desires are often rooted in emotions and, therefore, are easy to be redirected. For example, let's say you have a habit of eating junk food because when you do you feel a sense of comfort from eating it. In this case, your desire is for comfort, and your reward is experiencing that comfort. To redirect this reward, all you would need to do, then, is to identify healthier methods for achieving comfort. Perhaps you could identify comfort through listening to a guided meditation or relaxing music, through confiding in a trusted friend, or through massaging your body with a pleasant smelling lotion.

Anytime you are redirecting your reward, it is important that you understand exactly where that reward is being experienced in your life. Elaborating on comfort, for example, is the reward of comfort eating bringing you physical, mental, or emotional comfort? Or a combination of all three? When you begin to understand what specifically is being comforted, or rewarded, when you engage in habitual behavior, you gain the capacity to understand what specifically needs to be done to fulfill that reward in a new way.

Right now, I want you to take just one of the habits that you wish to change in your life. Then, I want you to write that habit down on the top of a piece of paper, or on a note in your phone. Under it, write down the cue and the step by step actions you are taking to fulfill that habit. Then, write down what you believe the reward is for fulfilling that habit. Now, I want you to write down all of the positive and negative side effects that you are experiencing in your life surrounding that particular habit. With all of this written down, you can now plainly see how this particular habit is serving you, how it is affecting you, and what benefit you are gaining from this habit that keeps you engaging in it time and again.

Now, I want you to brainstorm at least 3-5 different ways that you could fulfill this reward in a manner that is much healthier for you, and that will support you in achieving the results you desire. Be mindful of also identifying routines that will minimize unwanted or negative side effects so that you are not causing harm to yourself in any way whilst changing your existing habits. You will use this list of brainstormed routines to help you fully redirect your desire and habit in the next step.

Finding a Healthier New Routine

Finding a healthier new routine for any habit you have been engaging in for any period of time is important, and it takes some effort on your behalf. You need to adequately way the pros and cons of potential new routines so that you can see which ones are likely to give you the best benefits and which ones may keep you in a negative habit loop. At this point, your entire goal is to find a new routine that is going to give you a new experience with your old desire and reward. This way, you are able to continue to fulfill your needs without creating all of the unwanted side effects and patterns that your old routine was creating.

Once you have identified the best possible routine for you to engage in as a part of your new habit, you can write that routine down. Then, you want to break that routine down into a step-by-step process that you can follow in the same way and in the same order, every single time. Write that process down in order now so that you can see it out in front of you.

For the last part of redirecting your routine, you are going to want to honestly look through the routine to ensure that it will help you reach your desired goal. Then, you need to look through it and honestly assess whether or not this is a routine you will engage in. Consider your likes, dislikes, preferences, and personality, as well as what types of resources you have access to and whether or not this routine will actually fit in with your everyday life. You must make your new routine reasonable, realistic, and achievable in order for you to engage in it.

Otherwise, you are giving yourself every reason to stop engaging in it, rather than every reason to keep going.

The ideal routine for your redirected desires will be one that promotes your ability to fulfill your desire, achieve your reward, and do so in a way that has as few negative impacts on your life as possible. It should also be one that you are going to enjoy engaging in, that is going to be easy for you to engage in, and that will be sustainable for you to engage in. If your redirected routine fulfills all of these criteria, then you can feel confident that you have found a redirection that is going to maximize your potential to shift your bad habit for good.

Remaining Conscious Over Your Desires

You may have noticed I mentioned that no matter how effectively you create a new habit, or how long you engage in the new habit, it is possible that your old habit could emerge at any given point in an effort to achieve your desires and rewards the old way. This can happen anytime, an unrecognized cue is triggered, if the new habit has not been repeated enough to be strong enough to override the old habit, or if you are under stress and are suddenly in need of something familiar and comfortable. It can also happen if you begin to remove your conscious awareness from your habits, as you may find yourself slipping into old patterns unintentionally, and with no seeming rhyme or reason.

If you are going to effectively maintain your new habits and achieve your desired goals, you are going to have to remain conscious of your desires and your habits at all times. While this may seem counterintuitive, realize that this does not mean that you have to remove any level of automation from the new habits you have developed. You do not have to push yourself to consciously remember and engage in that habit over and over every single time. After all, it would not be a habit if you were engaging in this form of behavior.

Instead, your goal is to ensure that you are regularly consciously checking in with your habits and being mindful of your desires to ensure that your habits are continuing to fulfill your desires at all times. Over time, your desires may shift. As well, a change in your circumstances could give rise to new desires, or possibly even old desires that resurface. Being mindful and aware of this can support you in navigating your desires so that you can continue to empower and improve your positive habits and discourage and shift your negative habits. Through this, you will drastically minimize your risk of experiencing a relapse and falling out of your new habit.

Chapter 6

Planning Your New Habits

Shifting habits and creating new habits are quite similar, although the process does vary slightly. When it comes to shifting unwanted habits, your focus is on identifying your existing desire and reward and shifting the way that you fulfill that desire and reward. While it may seem like a new habit, you are still engaging in an old pattern; you are simply approaching it in a new way. Creating new habits altogether occurs when you uncover a new desire and the potential for a new reward and choose to develop a habit that will allow you to routinely fulfill that desire and reward. During this process, you truly do gain the opportunity to play master creator in your own life as you decide what your habits will look like and what lifestyle they will help you create.

Identifying the Need For New Habits

The first thing you must do when it comes to creating new habits is identifying the need for habits in the first place. When your brain automatically designs habits for you, it's number one focus is to identify what habits would optimize your daily or weekly experiences to ensure that you are able to get through them quickly and easily, every single time. Since you are taking the habit-making process off autopilot and putting it in your own hands, you are going to need to do this detective work for yourself to identify what habits are going to help you optimize your life.

In this unique scenario, you have the capacity to foresee how habits are going to affect you and, therefore, you can identify which habits are going to help you create the lifestyle you want rather than merely help you maintain the lifestyle you have. This gives you a sense of leverage in that you can identify and decide upon your chosen lifestyle in advance and then begin cultivating habits that will help you get there over time.

From this unique vantage point, you need to start identifying habits that are going to support you with cultivating the life that you actually want to be living, or developing the skills that will help you reach your desired goals. At this point, you can brainstorm some ideal habits that will help get you there, and you can break down that list and choose the one that you will start with based on what you think will get you the furthest. When it does come time to decide which one you will start with, make sure you only choose one as this is going to be your primary focus until you integrate it. Attempting to integrate too many new habits at once can be overwhelming for your brain, especially when these habits are designed with respect to what you anticipate or what you are creating, rather than what you are experiencing right now. Taking your time will ensure that you are able to be more thorough and that your new habits will be sustainable and effective.

The Anatomy Of a Positive Habit

With your list of potential habits brainstormed, it is time to start comparing those brainstormed habits to the anatomy of a positive habit. This way, you can identify which habit is going to be best suited to be your main focus for the coming weeks and possibly months as you place all your focus on the development and creation of this habit.

Positive habits should have these main elements: clarity, significance, low risk, simplicity, relevance, and desire. If these six elements are present in your ideal habit, you are looking at a habit that is likely going to support you in many ways as you begin to put it into action.

Clarity in a habit means that you can clearly identify what the habit is, what it will look like, and how it is going to benefit you. It should be simple for you to define the habit and each step of the habit itself to ensure that it is easy for you to follow and replicate. A habit that has not been clearly defined is one that may not provide you with the best results because you will not clearly understand what needs to be done. If you have only discovered the need for a habit, or for improvement in an area, but not an actual habit itself, you need to do more brainstorming.

Significance means that your new habit is going to offer you maximum impact, and as many benefits as possible. When we want to simplify something and integrate it as a part of our regular routine, it is important that we choose things that are going to go a long way. This does not mean that the biggest part of your day or the most important part of your goal needs to be turned into an automatic practice. It does, however, mean that the habit you are choosing to embrace is going to go a long way in helping you create results. For example, getting into the habit of making coffee before you start work every day is unlikely to affect your ability to achieve your goals, but getting into the habit of turning off distractions and getting focused will have a huge impact on your results. Make sure that the habits you choose will help create as many results for you as possible.

In addition to bringing you many benefits, you should also be focused on developing habits that are low risk. Habits are often considered a "bad" thing because many times we roll toxic behaviors into our habits, which in turn makes them bad. This is not inherent to habits, though, and the toxicity factor does not have to be relevant to every habit in existence. Make sure that any habit you create has as few risks as possible, and that it is not going to have detrimental or unwanted side effects that will ultimately negate from the point of the habit itself. If you do notice potential for something toxic to come of your new habit, adjust your habit to eliminate the risk.

Simplicity is a key factor in making any habit stick. The easier your habit is, the more likely you will be to see it all the way through and, therefore, the more success you will experience in developing that habit and truly turning it into an automatic behavioral pattern. Ideally, you should be able to clearly identify the process of the habit, and it should be effortless for you to access the resources and complete each step of that process.

The habits you are seeking to create should also be relevant to who you are and what you are and are not willing to do.

Attempting to create habits that are not relevant to you because they clash with your personality or your preferences is going to result in you struggling to see them all the way through. There are many ways to adapt habits so that they fit with your personality and preferences, and so that they are relevant to who you are and what you prefer. This way, you are creating habits that are realistic to you and that will actually get you the life that you desire and help you fulfill the goals that matter to you.

Lastly, you need to think about your desire factor around the habits you want to create. Remember, desire and reward are the number one things that drive us to create and maintain habits, and without them our habits will likely never stick. Identify which desire it is that is driving your potential habit and see if you can tie it in with a significant desire and a meaningful reward that will help you see your habit all the way through.

Giving Your Reward Significance

As desire is what drives the creation of habit, it is important that we address which desire it is that you are going to be tapping into, and what reward you are going to be using, to develop consistency within your habits. If you are going to be switching one habit for a new habit, all you need to do is change the routine while keeping the trigger and reward the same. If you are going to be creating an entirely new habit around an unexpressed desire, though, you are going to need to explore how to amplify that desire and create a strong enough reward to warrant the creation of a new habit.

By following the process of uncovering your desires in chapter 5, you have likely gained insight into what it is that you truly desire in your life. Through this, you can start to identify at least one strong desire you have that you can associate with your new habit and a potential reward that you can use alongside that desire to make that habit stick. In order to truly amplify the power of this desire, though, you need to teach your subconscious mind that it is a desire worth working toward. If you do not, your subconscious mind will ignore that desire because it does not know what it is missing.

A great way to get started with strengthening your desire and identifying a positive and strong reward for your new habit is to indulge in your unexpressed desires for a while. Try out new methods for pursuing and fulfilling those desires, and relish in the positive emotional and mental experience you have upon fulfilling them. Let yourself increase your desire through curiosity and exploration, and continue to do so until you find yourself incredibly excited about fulfilling that desire again and again. Then, turn that into a desire that drives your new habit.

By building up to the desire this way, you are training your brain to see that this particular desire is worth your attention, and that it is worth fulfilling. The subconscious then begins to realize that there is a positive intrinsic reward associated with this particular behavior and recognizes that a habit in this area of your life would be valuable. From there, when you begin to consciously implement intentional habits into this area of your life, you will have the support of your subconscious mind as it attempts to latch onto a habit in this area, too, so that it can continue to experience the desired reward.

Planning Out Your New Habit, Step-By-Step

Now that your subconscious mind is activated and ready to help your conscious mind implement your new habit, it is time for you to fit your new desired habit over the three step habit loop. You are going to start this process by identifying a simple, easy to identify the cue that will indicate when it is time to engage in your new habit. For example, a time of day, the ending of a different habit, or any other cue that you know without a doubt will reliably appear when you need it to in order to remind you to engage in your new habit.

After you have identified your cue, you need to go ahead and identify a simple to follow step-by-step method for the routine. Here, you need to clearly identify each part of the process you are going to follow, how, and in what order. It can be helpful to organize the steps of the process in chronological order on a checklist so that you can refer to it and complete the habit in the same way, and in the same order, every single time. Make sure this part is simple to follow and that it will be reasonable for you to complete each step the same way every time by ensuring that the necessary resources will be available for you to use.

Lastly, associate your routine with your reward by identifying how you will consciously tie your reward into the habit.

This could be through intentionally recognizing and indulging in the fulfillment of your desire as you engage in the habit and then exaggerating the reward when you receive it, or it could be through taking necessary action to draw forth the reward. Either way, make sure you clearly tie the routine into the reward so that you can guarantee its fulfillment every single time you engage in your habit. And, if possible, enhance the reward in a simple and repeatable manner so that you can increase your subconscious mind's desire to anchor in this new habit.

After you have identified the cue, routine, and reward for your habit loop, you are going to need to look your entire habit through from start to finish to ensure that it flows smoothly and effectively. If you notice any area of the habit that needs to be strengthened or reinforced, or that could be made simpler or more effective, work through that right away. You should also maintain some flexibility so that you can adapt your new habits as needed until you find the proper routine that works best for you.

Planning the Execution Of Your New Habit

The last step in planning your new habit before you can move into actual execution of that habit is to plan the execution itself. The execution of any new habit comes in two steps: the trial period and the official subscription. A trial period with a habit reflects the first few executions of the habit where you are trying out your plan for the habit and ensuring that it works, that it flows well, and that it gets you the results you desire. At this point, you are going to work through the habit a few times to ensure that you are getting exactly what you need out of it and that you are going to be able to engage in it over and over again for the foreseeable future.

The trial period of any new habit usually lasts for around the first 3-5 executions of the habit, as this is when you are really going to be going through the motions. At this point, you may realize that some of the steps you planned out need to be improved or that a step needs to be added or even removed in order for you to create the results that you desire. Be flexible during this time and be open to adapting your habit as needed, so long as the adaptation continues to help you achieve the results you desire.

Once you have effectively made it through the trial period, you will move into the subscription of the habit. This is where you officially subscribe to the method you have planned out for yourself, and you commit to seeing that habit through in the same way, and through the same order, time and again. At this point, you do not want to adjust the habit at all unless it is absolutely necessary, as doing so will result in you disrupting the natural habit making process in your subconscious mind. Remember, your subconscious mind does not care about good or bad; it cares about repetition. You want to repeat something as much as possible, and through that consistency, you will find yourself naturally integrating that habit into your life.

Through your continued subscription to your habit, you will find the habit slowly slipping into your subconscious mind until you no longer have to think about fulfilling that habit. Instead, it will automatically be fulfilled through the natural habit process of your subconscious mind. At this point, you will have completed your work with the habit, and all you will need to do is work toward maintaining that habit so that nothing in your life disrupts it or derails it. This is the part of the process where your habit fulfillment becomes virtually effortless and you can easily move on to creating and implementing another new habit to complement the one you have already implemented.

Chapter 7

Executing Your New Habits

While a great deal of the habit creation process revolves around rewards, anyone who has attempted to implement new habits into their lives will know that the reward is great, but it is virtually meaningless if you cannot get yourself started in the first place. Motivating yourself to begin a new habit or to engage in a new habit can be challenging, no matter how positive or rewarding you know it will be. That is because, arguably, you are in the habit of *not* engaging in that habit, and so you have to work toward breaking that cycle and getting into the action *as well as* get through the new habit. This may seem small in your conscious mind, but to your subconscious mind, that is a lot of work to sort through which is why it is so hard for you to get into action in the first place.

Fortunately, there are many things you can try to help you get motivated and get started so that you can leap into action and integrate your new habits. Each of these processes are designed to work *with* your nature, instead of against it, effectively supporting you with creating the motivation you need to engage in your new habits. As you approach these methods, it may be beneficial to turn the process of motivating yourself into a habit itself so that it becomes easier for you to continually engage in new habits. This can also help you draw away from the need for you to continually call on willpower so that you can stop exerting so much mental effort into the practice of getting motivated and start relying on a less mentally demanding experience.

Willpower and the Motivation To Engage

Willpower is a form of mental control that is exerted to help you do something or refrain from engaging in impulses. A great way to think of willpower is to consider it your mental turbo boost. When you are in need of that extra kick or mental strength, you can call on willpower to help get you through whatever it is that you are working through. With that being said, just like a turbo boost, it can only offer so much boost before it needs to recharge so that it can offer you more again in the future. In other words, relying on willpower for long periods of time is an ineffective and unsustainable way to approach your habits.

Rather than attempting to rely on willpower for long term support, it is more productive to rely on willpower to get you in the habit of getting started with your new habit. Use it to support you with creating the motivation to get started during the trial period and for the first few times that you work on your subscribed habit. Then, as you begin to move into a more full-time experience with your new habit, you can go ahead and start relying on other things to keep you going.

When you use willpower in this more sustainable method, you are leveraging it for what it is intended for rather than relying on it for more than it has the capacity to accomplish. In the meantime, as you use willpower to get you going, make sure that you are also supporting yourself in creating thoughts and beliefs that are going to keep you going so that you are fostering a positive can-do mindset toward your new habit.

Turning Motivation Into a Habit

When we address the creation of new habits, it can be easy to focus on the actual habit itself. For example, if you want to get into the habit of eating healthier, reading more, or exercising on a regular basis, you may focus exclusively on this new area of focus. However, if you really want to create sustainable results, it can be beneficial for you to focus on turning motivation into a habit, too. In fact, many people will focus on the habit of self-motivating before anything else, as this is a habit that can be relied on to create even more self-motivation in the future.

You can turn motivation into a habit by applying the same methods of habit creation to the habit of self-motivation, and by using that habit every single time, you need to motivate yourself to do something. Even if you are not motivating yourself to engage in a new habit per se, you can call on this habit to motivate you to mow the lawn, cook supper, or get a chore done that you have been putting off for a while now.

Each time you successfully motivate yourself to get something done, be sure to recognize your motivation and to emphasize your success that you experienced in motivating yourself to get into action. The more you can celebrate, amplify, and integrate this habit, the easier it will be to motivate yourself to begin new habits in the future as the process of even getting started with that new habit will bring a great sense of reward to your mind. In this way, you are creating smart habits that will go a long way in helping you achieve your goals.

Forming Your New Habits Around Existing Ones

During the trial period of your new habit, while you are still relying on willpower to get you started, it can be helpful to create other correlations that motivate you to get into action. These correlations begin to anchor into your subconscious mind that a habit needs to be engaged, which means that rather than relying on your willpower to get you started, you will feel a deeper need to engage in your habit due to the correlation itself. If you continue to create these correlations and act on them when you feel compelled to, you will effectively support your new habit with integrating into your subconscious mind. In other words, you will be supporting those early stages of creating and maintaining a new habit.

The best way to develop correlations to help you maintain your new habits is to create correlations that are easy to remember and follow. For example, attaching your new habit to an existing habit that you already have. This way, you are already up and in action, so moving into new action is easy because you do not need to summon the energy to get there. As well, at this point, your existing habit is already cemented in, and therefore, it is likely that you are going to engage in it no matter what. This way, you can feel confident that you are going to see it through and, therefore, you can feel confident that the cue to start your next habit will exist every single time.

To begin forming your new habit around existing ones, consider which habits will make the most sense to attach your new habits too. This way, you are organizing your habits in a way that makes sense and is reasonable, thus meaning you will be far more likely to see those habits all the way through. Make sure that the existing habit you choose is one that you have been doing for a long time, as attempting to attach a new habit to an immature habit can lead to you losing two habits rather than just one if you do find yourself falling off the wagon at any point. So, for example, attaching your new habit to a part of your morning, afternoon, or evening routine that you have had for a long period of time so that you are far more likely to actively engage in these new routines. When you build your schedule out wisely in this way, you are far more likely to see all of your habits through and create the results you desire.

Rewarding Yourself For Motivation

As you are turning motivation into a habit itself and calling on that habit to help you get into action on other habits you want to create, it is important that you consider the reward of this habit itself. In this case, you are going to be rewarding yourself for getting motivated to engage in your new habit *and* for completing the new habit, which means technically you will be experiencing two rewards to get you through the new habit you are engaging in.

The best way to reward yourself for motivation is to award your motivation efforts with your attention and awareness. In other words, every single time you motivate yourself into action focus largely on how proud you are of yourself and what you have been able to achieve in your life as a result of your motivation. Many times, people find themselves taking away from their own motivation rather than adding to it because as soon as they notice the need for motivation, or act on it, they flood their minds with negative thoughts. They think things like "I don't want to be doing this" or "this sucks" or "I can't wait until this gets easier," which tells their subconscious mind that engaging in this new habit is dreadful and that the reward is not worth it in the end. If, however, the thoughts you were flooding your mind with was positive, your brain would start to associate your new habit with positive things and, as a result, it would feel rewarded for getting motivated. This would start to formulate the positive foundation for your belief system that would then support your ability to move away from willpower and into habitual motivated action.

As you begin to cultivate new habits, start being particularly mindful around the mental dialogue you are experiencing anytime you go to engage in these habits, or as you are engaging in them. Be particularly cautious about any negative dialogue you are experiencing and mindfully move away from that negative dialogue anytime you find yourself engaging in it so that you can move toward positive dialogue instead.

You can also reward yourself for motivation through actual tangible rewards if you feel the need to ramp up your reward system. A quick little happy dance you do for yourself, or a few minutes spent singing or humming to your favorite song are great ways to show your mind that getting motivated is a great way to go. You can also try recognizing any tangible benefits from your motivation, such as having a completed task checked off of your to-do list, or some form of new extrinsic reward in your possession that you gained as a result of your motivation. By taking the extra moment to acknowledge and build excitement around these things, you work toward effectively rewarding yourself for getting motivated, which makes it even easier for you to get rewarded in the future.

Steps For Staying Consistent

Motivating yourself to get motivated is an important part of getting started with your new habits, but there is plenty more that you can be doing to help you stay consistent with your new habits, too. The more actions you can take to help yourself stay motivated, the more likely you will be to get into action and complete your new habit every single time. This way, you will have a much easier time integrating this new habit into your subconscious mind, effectively making it a real habit.

One of the best ways that you can stay consistent with your new habit is to have some sort of alarm or reminder set that will tell you when it is time to engage in your new habit. If you find that you are the type of person who tends to put reminders off until a later time, you might consider putting a few on just to make sure that you really do get up and get into action. Oftentimes, when we engage in new habits, it can be easy to completely forget about said habit until it begins to develop some level of automation. This is because you are simply not used to engaging in the habit and so it is incredibly easy for the habit itself to slip your mind. If you were to have a reminder, however, you would not have to worry about forgetting to engage in the habit because you would already have the reminder you need to get started.

Another great way to help yourself stay consistent is to motivate yourself to get into the habit of keeping everything as simple as possible. For example, make sure that all of the supplies you need to complete your habit are readily available, easy to access, and easy to use. This way, when it comes time for you to engage in your new habit, you are less likely to make any excuses or complain because you already have everything you need in place to help you get started.

Another way that you can help yourself stay consistent with new habits is through a personal accountability system that acts as a form of reward all on its own. To understand what I mean, think back to when you were a child, and recall how people used to motivate you to see things through. It is likely that your parents or teachers used things like stickers as a little reward to help you stay motivated to get something done. This way, the reward of actually seeing the new habit through was amplified by the reward of the sticker or the other accountability method. Creating these accountability methods for yourself is a great way to amplify your motivation, add an extra layer of rewards, and keep yourself on track.

If you do choose to use a personal accountability system, you should be cautious about how you approach periods where you fail to see your new habits. With these systems, it can be easy to start to feel bad and get down on yourself if you miss a few days, but that is actually the worst way to approach your new habit when you have made the mistake of breaking your consistency. Rather than getting down on yourself and making yourself feel bad for not seeing that habit through, you would be better to acknowledge anytime you have not been seeing your habit through and use willpower to get yourself moving forward again. If you find that this alone is not enough, you can sit and brainstorm why you do not see your habit through and what needs to change in order for you to get back into action with it. The more you can continue to address and adjust your habit when this happens, the more likely you will be to create a habit that is easy for you to see all the way through. As you do this, be sure to keep a positive or, at the very least, neutral mindset toward your ability to fulfill your habit as bullying yourself or being negative toward yourself will only further deter you from getting back into the habit of your new habit!

Chapter 8

How To Pamper a Habit (and Why)

New habits are high maintenance, no matter what you do to try to make them easier. While there are many ways that you can make your new habits more approachable or simpler for you to embrace, there is nothing you can do to entirely erase the fact that new habits require effort and work on your behalf. The sooner you can accept this, the sooner you can begin to discover how you can nurture your new habits so that they are more likely to stick.

Pampering a new habit essentially means that you are going to acknowledge the fragility of this new habit, recognize that it is easier for you to drop this habit if you are not careful, and then do everything in your power to nurture the habit. The more you can continue to nurture this habit, the more likely you will be to find yourself maintaining consistency so that you can see this habit all the way through to becoming a true habit.

Rest assured that while pampering a new habit does mean that you are going to put added effort into maintaining your new habit, it does not mean that you are going to be babying your habit forever. It simply means that until your habit is rock-solid and less likely to fall apart, you will continue to nurture this new habit and remain mindful of it so that you can feel absolutely confident that you will be able to see this habit all the way through.

Why New Habits Will Always Be More Fragile

New habits are incredibly fragile when you first take them on, and they remain fragile for quite some time after that. While their level of fragility will slowly decline over time, it is important to note that even after years of engaging in a habit, it is still at risk of being abandoned for a habit that has been around for much longer than that habit has been. The more mindful you can be of this fact, the more you can prevent yourself from sabotaging the new habit or losing it in favor of an older and more deeply embedded habit.

The fragility of new habits largely comes from the fact that your brains neuropathways are much stronger for habits that have been around longer, or that have been anchored in deeper. These stronger neuropathways are far more likely to be executed than the more fragile and fresh neuropathways of your younger habits, as your brain can guarantee their results. Plus, they are so worn in that your brain can execute them easily without having to exert too much effort. As a result, they are preferred over newer habits.

If you do not develop the mindfulness of this fact and instead rely on your subconscious mind to help you navigate your habits, it is likely that your new habits will be canceled entirely in favor of older habits that your brain deems as being more effective. As a result, you will constantly find yourself breaking new habits in favor of old ones and struggling to recreate any new habits. While the ones you have worked to create will be easier to recreate than even newer ones, they will still be more fragile than the ones that have been around longer.

Over time, your newer habits will have existed long enough that they will count as older habits and, as a result, they will not be quite so fragile compared to other habits you have been working on creating. However, any habits you have consciously created will always be at risk of being canceled in favor of older habits if you are not careful. If you recall, there are typically countless cues that indicate when a habit should be acted on and, when you consciously create habits, it can be hard to identify and adjust the habits surrounding every single cue your subconscious mind has picked up on. In fact, it may be downright impossible as you cannot examine your subconscious mind to identify what is inside of it. Furthermore, the cues it picks up on are often ones that fall beyond your conscious awareness and could include anything from a certain smell or voice to a certain time of day or emotion you experience. This makes navigating and deleting or rewiring your cues nearly impossible, meaning that you must always be mindful of your habits to avoid accidentally slipping into old patterns and canceling new ones.

What Happens When You Don't Pamper a Habit

When you don't pamper a new habit, it shows. The simplest way to identify a lack of pampering with a new habit is to look for the habits that disappeared as quickly as they appeared. This is because, eventually, the willpower-based momentum that supported these habits in coming to the surface stopped, and the habit was abruptly canceled when your brain then decided to rely on an old habit. Since you were unlikely to be aware of why this was happening, or what you should do about it, you may have found yourself navigating this situation feeling as though you failed yourself or your new habit when, in reality, you simply did not know how to work with the nature of your subconscious mind.

New habits that are canceled due to a lack of pampering can be witnessed as having been cancelled at any phase during their creation. They could be cancelled within days, weeks, months, or even years of being created. For example, let's say you got into the habit of waking up and exercising when you were living abroad, but as soon as you returned home three years later, you abruptly stopped exercising in the morning and now it is challenging for you to start again. Or, let's say you were eating healthier for three months and then you abruptly stopped and went right back to your old eating patterns. These abrupt stops happened because something triggered your old patterns and, you not being aware of what was going on, had no way of knowing how to navigate these situations mindfully.

When you learn how to pamper a habit, you learn how to spot weaknesses in your habit, as well as identify possible situations that could prevent you from effectively navigating and maintaining your habit. Through this, you find yourself being able to mindfully navigate all weaknesses and situations that may cause you to cancel your habit so that, instead, you can strengthen it and keep it alive and thriving.

The goal here, then, is not to turn your habit into anything high maintenance or that will require a long period of ongoing effort and attention so that you can keep it running. After all, this would be no different than trying to run a habit on willpower rather than subconscious power, which we already know is ineffective. Instead, your goal is to simply be mindful of all of your habits and continue to navigate them as intentionally as possible during periods where they may be jeopardized so that your brain never cancels them in favor of an old pattern.

What It Looks Like To Pamper a Habit

To pamper a habit means to shower it with attention and intention and to keep your focus on maintaining that habit for as long as it takes for that habit to become automatic. This means that you are going to remain dedicated to the habit and that you will do anything you need to in order to see it through and fulfill it every single day. You may even go so far as to doing research to identify new ways to improve your habit, maintain your habit, or even develop smaller "side habits" to help you maintain this habit even more effectively.

In addition to remaining as dedicated to seeing the habit through as you possibly can be, you will also use some of your conscious awareness to ensure that you are doing everything in your power to support that habit. This means you are going to do the extra little bit to ensure that everything is organized so that it is easier for you to do the habit when the time comes. It also means that you are going to continually analyze to ensure that you are doing it properly and to the best of your ability, and that should you notice any weaknesses or setbacks in the development of your habit, you will do what you can to improve the situation.

Should you find yourself experiencing any sort of setback with your habit, you will immediately begin to pamper that habit once more and will jump right back into action as though you never missed a beat. When you are truly pampering a habit, there is no time to sit around and wish you had not quit or to get down on yourself for not keeping up with your habit. This would mean that you had accepted defeat and that you had decided to permanently give up your habit. Instead, you acknowledge the habit has taken a stumble, and you immediately work toward finding a way to repair that stumble by identifying what went wrong and fixing the circumstances. This way, you are not accepting defeat over your habit, but rather, you are staying committed to seeing the habit all the way through, effectively pampering your habit.

While you will not need to pamper a habit quite so long, the longer you maintain it, you will need to continue to pamper it for as long as you wish to have that habit. Over time, however, the habit will require less and less of your attention as you become more capable of engaging in it in a subconscious way. Even so, you should be prepared to check in on your habit from time to time to ensure that it is continuing to work for you and that you are continuing to follow it in the best way possible. If you find yourself slipping, recognize a need for it to be improved, or realize that you have stopped engaging with it altogether, this would be the best time to reinforce that habit and place a greater focus in it so that you can continue maintaining it long term.

How To Pamper Your Own Habit

As far as pampering your own habit goes, there are a few things that you need to consider. If you are going to effectively pamper your habit enough to ensure that it sticks and you do not end up with a canceled habit, you are going to need to put effort into making sure that you have a plan in place for *how* you are going to pamper that habit.

Each habit is designed differently with different cues, routines, and rewards, and different purposes. For that reason, it is best to ensure that you address each unique habit and create plans for how you are going to measure your level of success with that particular habit. Once you have identified how you are going to be able to address and measure each habit, you are going to want to create a plan for how you are going to keep up with these measurements. This way, you know exactly what to expect as far as how you are going to need to manage your new habit to keep it active and effective.

Since you want to focus all of your energy into actually building the habit, it is useful to put your pampering methods on autopilot so that you are not in need of adding any additional habits into your life. Ideally, you should put reminders in your phone to check in on how your habit is doing so that you can receive these reminders automatically. This way, all you need to do is sit down and mindfully think about how the habit is going each time a reminder goes off. You could also use that moment to get everything ready so that it is easier for you to engage in the habit itself when the time comes. At first, you may want to have these reminders scheduled daily. Once you start to notice the habit getting easier and easier, though, you can start to set the reminders a few days apart, and then weekly, and then every few weeks. Eventually, you may only need to check in with your habits on a month to month basis to ensure that everything is running smoothly. During these periodic check ins, you may even check in on multiple habits at once to ensure you are continuing to create the results you desire. Then, if you find that you are not, you can take the necessary measures to begin pampering your habit all over again.

Being Mindful Of High Stress Periods

One of the most important elements of effectively pampering a habit is being able to anticipate periods where you are likely to stop engaging with your habits. Knowing how to anticipate when you are going to experience stress or overwhelm that could throw your habits off means that you can create measures in advance that will prevent you from having your entire system thrown for a loop. This way, you can mindfully navigate these high stress periods or periods of change in such a way that allows you to continue to maintain your habits to the best of your ability. Then, as everything begins to settle again, you can start to go back to only checking in on your habits casually.

It is important to understand that periods of high stress can interrupt habits of any magnitude, no matter how long you have had them or how meticulous you are at engaging in those habits. Some things to look for include: large moves, changes in your lifestyle, job changes or transitions, or changes to your relationship status or family, such as with the introduction of a new family member in the household. High stress periods such as those when you are experiencing heightened pressure from work or your personal life, those where you may be facing issues with your health, or those where you may be facing any other types of stress even if it does not seem all that significant can also impact your ability to maintain your habits.

Anytime you recognize yourself going through one of these phases, be sure to immediately address your habits and consider what you are going to do to ensure that you continue to maintain them to the best of your ability. You may even find that you need to adapt them for a period to ensure that they serve your needs during periods of stress or change. The more mindfully you do this, the more likely you will be to maintain the changes and refrain from developing bad and difficult-to-change habits during periods of stress.

Chapter 9

Making Habits As Simple As Possible

One of the best things you can do for yourself when it comes to making new habits is making habits that are as simple as they can possibly be. When habits are simple, it is easier to motivate yourself to get started with that habit, and it can also be easier for you to see that habit all the way through. This way, rather than having to train yourself to complete a series of complex steps in a specific order, you can focus on practicing simple steps, or you can simplify complex things to make them easier for you to remember.

When it comes to habit creation, there will be some situations where you can easily simplify the process, and there will be others while simplification will not be so simple. For example, you may be able to simplify your morning routine, but you may not be able to simplify certain processes at work, which may need to be done in a specific way. In this case, the best thing you can do is simplify the process to the best of your ability to ensure that you are getting everything done properly.

In situations where you do have more control, learning how to make things as easy as possible will help shed away the need to exert unnecessary energy, as well as the need to attempt to remember complex processes. It can be natural to want to make things more challenging if you believe the added few steps will get you greater results, but the reality is that those added few steps may make the habit unreasonable when it comes to executing it day in and day out. If those steps are absolutely necessary, or they really will have a huge impact, you can always add them into the habit at a later date, once you are in the habit of the basic practice itself, first.

In situations where you have no control over how things are done, you can develop habits by simplifying what you can and by starting with just a few habits here and there while continuing to do everything else intentionally. Over time, you can add more habits into your "base habits" to make it even easier for you to create the results you desire over time. Doing it this way will ensure that it is easier for you to create true habits and the results you desire with those habits.

Effective Methods For Simplifying Your Habits

Choosing how to simplify your habits is going to depend on whether you are simplifying a brand new habit that you are creating for yourself or one that you have already been engaging in for some time. In both cases, you are going to need to put your detective skills to work and analyze the routine aspect of your habit to ensure that it is as simple and easy-to-follow as possible.

For habits that you already have, simplifying them can be a great way to adjust the routine to ensure that you are still getting your desired reward fulfilled, but that you are also not expending any unnecessary energy in doing so. Sometimes, when we have habits for a long period of time, it can be easy to overlook ways that we are wasting energy by doing things that are not necessary with those habits. For example, you might still be following an outdated system for filing your invoices at work because that is the habit you are in when, by now, there is a much quicker and easier way of doing it. Simplifying your habits whenever possible, even long-time habits is a great way of ensuring that you are never wasting energy when it is not needed.

As you begin to create new habits for yourself, it is also a good idea to look through those new habits to see how you might be able to simplify them. In particular, pay attention to the routine itself and see if there is anything you can do to make the routine easier, to make it pack a bigger punch, or to help it do both. Do your best to look at your routine from a practical standpoint, too, and see if it flows effectively. Sometimes when we are in the planning process of things, it can be easy to get carried away with how things *could* be and we find ourselves forgetting how they *are*. Ensure that your simplified plan is realistic. Otherwise, you are going to have a hard time seeing it through. While you will certainly be able to work out the kinks during your trial period, you do not want to have so much to sort out that it is challenging to even get through the trial period of your new habit in the first place.

If you are unsure about how a routine might be simplified, try researching similar habits that people have. These days, there are countless self-help blogs full of different habits people have that contain plenty of great details about what those habits are and how they look. Getting an idea of how other people are navigating their habits can be a great way to identify new opportunities to create and simplify your own.

How To Ensure That You Still Get Your Desired Results

As you simplify your habits, it is important that you do not simplify it to the point where you no longer get your desired results out of the habit. After all, this would be a waste of your time and would render the habit completely useless. Your goal whenever you are navigating the creation of a habit should always be to create the biggest impact through the fewest steps possible. The more you can master this balance, the better your habits will be, and the greater your impact will be toward reaching your goals through your habit.

The perfect way to ensure that your habits are still functional after you have simplified them is to compare them to your goals and see if you can realistically see how your habits are going to take you toward your goals. If it seems like they will do so in a positive and powerful manner, you have likely done an effective job of making your habit simplified while still being able to reach your goals. If, however, it seems as though your goal will be unreachable, you will want to adjust your habit to ensure that you can make a meaningful impact. After all, the entire purpose of this book is to create habits that are going to help you reach your goals!

Chapter 10

How To Break Bad Habits

Bad habits are something that every single one of us is familiar with, and something we have all wanted to break at one point or another. Dealing with bad habits can be frustrating, troublesome, and even overwhelming or embarrassing. If we are not careful, they can also overrule our lives and leave us living a lifestyle that we truly do not want to be living, all because we have felt committed to or trapped within bad habits.

It may seem impossible to break your bad habits, especially if you have been living with them for a long period of time, but rest assured that like any habit, a bad habit can be broken. The number one reason why most people *don't* break their bad habits is that their mindset surrounding their bad habits is one that makes it seem as though change is impossible and improbable. As a result, they lack the mental strength they need to see the trial period through and get into the process of truly changing their bad habits. If you can shift this belief system within yourself and empower yourself to change your bad habits, then you will see yourself effectively breaking free from every single bad habit you may experience in your life.

Getting Real With Yourself About Bad Habits

The first thing you need to do when it comes to dealing with your bad habit is getting real with yourself about them. Start by acknowledging that they are bad habits, that you are responsible for them, and that you need to be responsible for changing them. Now, you need to start to acknowledge what your mindset is like around your bad habits. More often than not, you will notice that your mindset is disempowered and full of beliefs that leave you feeling as though you have no control or say over the matter. This very mindset is what makes navigating the process of breaking your bad habits so hard because you have given them so much power and control that it feels as though there is nothing you can do to change the situation.

If you are going to find the strength to break apart bad habits and eliminate them for good, you are going to have to first address your mindset around these bad habits so that you can take back your power. This way, you will genuinely believe in yourself and in your ability, and through that your subconscious mind will begin to pay attention and support you with creating the results you need when it comes to eliminating these habits.

As soon as you have identified your mindset around your bad habits, you need to start empowering yourself to believe that it is possible for you to break these habits and find new ones that will serve you in a bigger way. The best way to get started with these is to get real about your bad habits and put some perspective around them. Notice that your bad habit is likely not nearly as bad as you make it out to be and that it doesn't really need to be that big of a deal in your life. Rather than giving your bad habit any emotional charge, see it as just being an experience you are having that you are ready to change so that you can have an experience that is more useful to you. It may take some time for you to make this adjustment in your beliefs and emotions, so do not be afraid to give yourself time to navigate this shift in your mindset.

Once you start to see your bad habit through a neutral perspective, you need to start building up your belief in your ability to create new habits. At this point, you want to avoid focusing on the bad habit as much as possible and instead focus on what positive you can create in your life. Focus on how easy it can be for you to create new habits, how fun it can be to try new things, and how much better your results and rewards will be when you try these new habits. You can also start looking around for evidence about how effectively other people have broken habits similar to yours to realize that it is entirely possible, and it is well within your ability to do so.

Your entire goal at this point is to take away any attention and focus you give to your bad habit and start focusing entirely on new habits and your potential and power. Stop listening to people who say you can't, or people who make it seem like bad habits are inevitable, unavoidable, and unfixable, and start listening to people who tell you that it is possible and who gives you guidance to support you along the way. As you continue to make this shift in your mindset that focuses less on getting away from your bad habit and more on moving toward your healthier habits, you will find that it becomes easier and easier for you to make shifts in your life. That is because, to put it simply, whatever you focus on grows.

Fitting a New Routine Over Your Habit

Once you have navigated the practical mindset aspect of breaking your bad habits by eliminating any negative beliefs you are carrying around them, you can begin to focus on the actual breaking down of the habit itself. At this point, you can start following the same steps from previous chapters in this book to create change in your habits. To do this, you will want to identify the cue and reward associated with your formerly bad habit and start focusing on effective routines you can use to navigate your new habit.

This way, you are able to break up the habit and create new results for yourself.

Remember, your goal should be to maintain your cues and rewards but focus solely on changing your routine, as this is where your power lies. The less you try to fight against desire and nature, and the more you can focus on working with your existing nature, the more effectively you will be able to break your bad habits.

As you create your new routine to replace your habit, it is imperative that you are thoughtful and considerate about the routine you plan. Realize that with all habits, the routine is important and carries a great weight around whether or not you will be able to integrate it as a habit. By replacing bad habits, however, the routine is extremely important as you have built up a significant belief system suggesting that it is not possible for you to change your habit. Even if you have been doing work to shift your belief system, pairing that with a meticulously planned routine that will promote your success will ensure that you have far higher chances of creating success with this changed habit in the first place.

Be sure to follow all of the standard practices of clearly defining the routine, breaking it down into simple-to-follow chronological steps, and making it as simple and thorough as possible so that you are more likely to follow it. If you can, you should also put measures into place to prepare yourself for any emotional or mental setbacks you may have that could prevent you from engaging with the changed habit. This way, you are far more prepared to handle the emotional and mental challenges that may be presented from attempting to get through this particular habit change.

Mindfully Navigating the Breakdown Of Your Bad Habit

As you begin to break down a bad habit and transform it into something positive, it is important that you are mindful of navigating this process. Bad habits in and of themselves tend to be harder to break, particularly because of the intense connection they can have to your belief system, values, and emotions. Knowing what to expect and navigating these situations mindfully is an important way to help yourself get through the harder mental and emotional parts of breaking down bad habits. When you can mindfully navigate these parts of the process, you can release yourself from the idea that the suffering you experience will be unbearable or will last forever, allowing you to experience a greater sense of peace during this process. Most often, this peace and the realization that the discomfort and any suffering associated with breaking bad habits will end minimizes the suffering and ensures that it passes much quicker.

Realize that the first week of changing a bad habit is usually the hardest week. This is the week where you are going to be navigating strong cravings or urges to engage in your old habit, and you may struggle to feel any level of fulfillment or satisfaction from your new habit. Even if it is designed to fulfill the same reward and need, you will find yourself feeling as though the need itself is not fulfilled because it has not been fulfilled in the way that you are used to having it fulfilled. It will take some time for your subconscious mind to acknowledge that the same need is being fulfilled, just in a different way. You are also going to navigate many firsts during this week, including several cues that will go unfulfilled because of your conscious choice to switch your habit to something different. This first week can bring about great emotional and mental frustrations and even distress as you find yourself getting used to this new normal.

The second and third week into this process, you will find yourself slowly beginning to relax, although it will still be challenging. At this point, you may begin to feel more at peace with your new habit, but you will continue to experience a heightened risk of backsliding into your old ways. The more relaxed you feel about your new habit, the more at risk you become, so it is important that you navigate this time mindfully to refrain from experiencing a setback. At this point, cues are going to continually arise and trigger the old habit, and if you are too relaxed, you may engage in it accidentally, or find yourself in a position where the emotional and mental urge to engage in it are too strong and it feels impossible to deny it.

As time goes on, you will continue to feel random periods of emotional and mental frustration surrounding your changed habit, but it will grow easier and easier. Still, you must always be cautious as you never know when an old cue will be unexpectedly presented, potentially causing room for a setback. The more mindful you can be of this possibility, the more you can navigate these situations in such a way that it will not cause you to slip back into old patterns.

It is also important to realize that this timeline is merely a guideline for what to expect. How you experience this will ultimately depend on you, your personality, the unique habit you are breaking, and many other variables that may be outside of your control. Still, the more mindfully you can navigate this, the more success you will have in completely breaking down your old habit and replacing it with a new one.

Chapter 11

Habits You Should Have

Working together to develop stronger habits for you to reach your goals has me wanting to impart wisdom on what goals have supported me in reaching my own goals over the years. These habits have proven to support me in my ability to stay motivated, get everything done, and see things through so that I am able to achieve the results I desire. Including these habits in your own day to day experience can help you experience greater success with your habits, too, while also supporting you in achieving your own goals.

Some of these habits may seem generic, so I want to underline something important. Each of us, no matter how unique we may be in personality and expression, has a basic set of needs that our bodies and minds require to be fulfilled in order for us to do anything. If these basic needs are not fulfilled, we may find ourselves falling into default and unconscious patterns as a way to fulfill them, which can result in us taking up habits that take away from our ability to either consciously or habitually reach our goals.

The more you can learn how to incorporate these habits into your everyday life, the more effectively you will be able to support yourself in creating a solid foundation for you to generate success. In many cases, these habits alone will amplify your success in a way that no other habit can. As well, developing new habits that are specific to you, your needs, and your desires will become a lot easier once you have these habits in place. So, it is well worth it to research these habits and discover how you can implement them in your own life in a way that fulfills your own needs.

Getting Up Early Each Morning

While there is a lot of speculation around how early you should wake up in order to have a successful day, I don't believe there is one golden hour that will fit everyone. Instead, I believe that each of us has our own hour that serves as the best time for when we should rise every single day. Finding your "golden hour" can be done by identifying how much sleep you need in order to feel rested, discovering how much time you need in order to get your day started every single day, and figuring out what generally feels right for you. You may want to play around with your waking hour for a little while until you find what feels best.

Once you have found your "golden hour," aim to awaken at that time every single day, regardless of what you have going on for that day. This way, you can start every single day off right, ready for whatever may come your way. Plus, if any great opportunities to make advancements toward your goals present themselves, you can take advantage of them as you are in the perfect frame of mind to turn them into a success.

Giving Gratitude For Each Day

Gratitude is a powerful emotion that can literally rewire your brain and set you up for success. People who approach their lives from a point of gratitude tend to be more positive, open minded, and curious about life itself. When they are presented with new opportunities, rather than immediately worrying about whether or not they are capable of fulfilling those opportunities or becoming skeptical about the quality of the opportunities, they accept them with gratitude. Then, through gratitude, they generate a level of belief in themselves that enables them to embrace and utilize those opportunities to their advantage.

Creating a habit surrounding gratitude in your everyday life is a great way to help provide you with these same benefits so that you, too, can create a sense of positivity and optimism in your own life. A great gratitude habit you could include in your life is one that can be included in your day immediately upon waking up. As soon as you awaken, express gratitude for 3-5 things that you are grateful for in your life. Try to choose something new every day so that you have to consciously think about what it is that you want to express gratitude for, as this will allow you to create a stronger sense of gratitude. Watch how this simple habit drastically shifts your mindset and, as a result, your life.

Making a List Of Your Goals

Although many of us can recite what our goals are, very few of us write those goals down and turn them into plans that we are working toward. There is something profoundly impactful about writing your goals down on paper and reviewing those goals every single day. In fact, some people, such as Grant Cardone, will write their goals down every single time they are feeling doubtful, uncertain, or unmotivated, as this enables them to get back into the mindset of remembering what it is that they are working toward. This way, they can stay motivated and keep going.

Rather than holding onto your goals in your mind, turn them into something tangible. Write your goals down on paper and review that piece of paper every single morning, and anytime you find yourself feeling uncertain, doubtful, insecure, or unmotivated. The more you can refresh yourself on these goals, the more motivated you will remain to reach them in your everyday life.

Exercising Daily

Your body is an important part of you, and if you fail to take care of it, you will find yourself struggling to fulfill your goals largely due to the fact that you are in too ill of health to be able to pursue them. Rather than letting your health fall to the wayside and finding yourself too ill to pursue your goals, take your health seriously. Exercise for at least 30 minutes every single day, even if you are not capable of engaging in intense exercise. Walking, jogging, biking, swimming, yoga or even doing at-home cardio workouts are all great ways to get your body moving on a daily basis.

There are countless studies that show how your body thrives when you take proper care of it, so doing this is important. If you are someone who has never had a consistent workout routine or who struggles to work out on a regular basis, you might consider working together with an accountability partner or a personal trainer until you get into the swing of things. Once working out comes more naturally to you, you can adjust your plan as needed.

Eating a Healthy Diet

In addition to taking care of your body through movement, it is also important to take care of your body through nutrition. Eating is about far more than just satiating a hunger craving that you get a few times a day. Eating is about learning which foods are going to nour

ish you best so that your brain, organs, and body are all able to function at maximum capacity. Highly successful people know that the better they can nourish themselves, the better they will be able to get through their day to day lives.

If cooking or preparing food is not something you enjoy, find a dietary guide that looks tasty for you and teach yourself how to master a few recipes from that dietary guide. Then, rely on the habit of being able to make this food as a way to help yourself eat healthy on a routine basis. You might also try meal prepping as a way to prepare healthy food for yourself, as this is another great way to nurture your body and take care of your wellbeing.

Managing Your Money Properly

Many people believe that they are bad with money, or that they are experiencing a level of lack or poverty because of reasons that are beyond themselves. While this may be true, there are also countless other people who are relying on these two reasons as excuses when, in reality, they could be experiencing far greater success with their funds. All they need to do is get out of the habit of spending all their money so that they can get into the habit of saving and investing their money.

The more effective you are at managing funds, the more successful you will be at saving money so that you can allocate those funds toward things that are more meaningful to you, such as retirement or large purchases like cars and homes. Get into the habit of budgeting your money every month and sticking to that budget meticulously throughout the month. Stop engaging in habits that result in you spending pointless money throughout the month, too, such as purchasing your coffee from a drive-thru rather than making it at home, or eating out because you are too lazy to cook. These simple shifts can go a long way in helping you make your funds go further, which can create security, comfort, and an added ability to reach your goals.

Keeping a Precise Agenda

Your time is the most precious resource you have, precious even more so than the funds in your bank account. Rather than wasting all of your time engaging in habits that do not add to the quality of your life, start taking your time seriously and keeping a precise agenda. The more effectively you can schedule your time and stick to that schedule, the more effectively you will be able to get through the day and reach all of your goals.

Start keeping an agenda with you, and every time you agree to do something make sure you schedule it into your agenda. Then, make sure you spend time each month, week, and day scheduling out how your time is going to be spent so that you know exactly what you need to be doing and when. The more you can get into the habit of keeping track of your time and directing your time meticulously, the more you will get done on a day to day basis. This way, rather than sitting around doing nothing, you are intentionally using up every minute of your time to support yourself in achieving your goals.

Enjoying an Hour To Yourself

It is important to educate yourself on the difference between wasting time and investing time into yourself. Many people feel like sitting around enjoying time by themselves is time wasted because they are not productive. On the contrary, spending time on your own, even if that time is spent staring at the ceiling being bored, can actually be incredibly supportive of your mental and emotional health. This time is a great opportunity for you to enjoy your company, unwind, process any residual thoughts or emotions you may be carrying with you, and otherwise take a good moment to relax.

Get into the habit of spending an entire hour to yourself every day, or as close to an hour as you possibly can. During this hour, do whatever feels good for you, and notice how much it transforms your mental and emotional health. There is a great deal of benefit that can come from giving yourself absolute permission to enjoy time by yourself, knowing that you are not putting anything off and that your day is not suffering based on your decision.

Checking In With Yourself Each Evening

Making the mistake of carrying your day with you to bed can create heightened stress, reduced quality of sleep, and long term mental health struggles as you find this day to day stress compounds and feels worse over time. Rather than carrying everything with you to the pillow, set aside some time for yourself to check in with how you are doing. This time in the evening spent releasing your thoughts and emotions, and bringing closure to your day will help you go to sleep feeling peaceful, which will allow you to feel well rested and ready for a wonderful day ahead.

If sitting and simply thinking is not enough for you, you can incorporate other routines into this nightly check in, too. Consider meditating, engaging in a calming yoga session, journaling, or drinking a calming tea as you enjoy this time to relax your mind and release the weight of the day so that you can rest deeply and thoroughly later that night. If, during this time, you realize that you wished something had gone differently during the day or that something was left incomplete, make a note of it and take care of it the next day.

Reading For 30 Minutes Before Bed

Studies have shown that anything you learn in the 30 minutes before bed is learned faster because of how your brain processes information as you sleep. With this information, we can assume that what we think about before we go to bed is tremendously important, and choosing our thoughts intentionally can go a long way toward helping us not only learn but also feel better. Use the 30 minutes you have before going to sleep as an opportunity to educate yourself on skills that could support you with achieving any goals you are working toward in your life. This way, you are learning information that is conducive to your growth and your success. While some people prefer to read in bed, I suggest reading next to a lamp on a chair or the sofa in your living room. This way, your mind associates your bed only with sleeping and when your head hits the pillow you are able to fall asleep quicker and easier.

Chapter 12

Habits You Should Quit

Just like you are going to want to pick up new habits that will help you navigate a healthier life, there are also some bad habits that you should consider eliminating from your life so that you can pursue your goals even more effectively. For me, there have been many habits that I have had to eliminate from my life so that I can experience greater success. Although it seemed hard to break these habits at the time, I have come to realize how powerfully my life has changed since I left them behind. Plus, over time, it does get much easier to go without these habits, meaning that the suffering and discomfort does end.

If you have any of these habits in your life or any others that you can clearly observe as having a negative impact on your life and your ability to reach your goals, you are going to want to recognize these goals and begin eliminating them from your life. With that being said, I recommend only working toward breaking one bad habit as a time, as trying to break too many can be overwhelming. While focusing on one at a time means the others may linger for a while longer, it also means that your ability to eliminate them will be far more sustainable and likely to remain permanent, which will have a far more positive impact for you in the long run.

Smoking

Smoking is a habit that comes with many obvious negative side effects. From damaging your health to draining your wallet, smoking can seriously set you back. For most people, smoking is either a way of getting some quiet time to themselves, a way of navigating stress, or both. If you can learn how to fulfill these needs in other, healthier ways, letting go of smoking will become much easier for you.

With that being said, smoking is an addiction that includes a dependency on a substance that you are introducing to your body. For this reason, smoking will be a harder habit for you to break. As you are working on breaking the habit in your subconscious mind, you will also need to navigate the physical detox you will go through at the same time. This combined experience of denying pleasure while willingly choosing pain can be incredibly difficult to navigate, so you are going to want to take your time and do so intentionally. It may be useful to buy a smoking cessation book, join a program, or work with your doctor to increase your ability to successfully navigate breaking this bad habit.

Biting Your Nails

Biting your nails, or any other habits that are borne out of nervousness, such as sucking your hair, picking at your skin, or chewing your lips, are all habits that need to be rectified. These habits are often developed as a way to experience a positive release from negative emotions through the form of self-soothing. They can also indicate to your brain that there is a reason to be nervous in the first place, even if there is not, which can worsen your nervousness and, in turn, worsen your habit as well.

Rather than letting these self-mutilating habits continue, it can be helpful to learn how to self-soothe in other ways so that you are more likely to experience a positive release from negative emotions, rather than a release that actually worsens these emotions. Consider trying things like talking, humming to yourself, journaling, distracting yourself for a few minutes, meditating, mindfully breathing, or grounding, which are all healthier ways to combat nervousness in a positive and healthy manner.

Sleeping In

Sleeping in is a bad habit that you can get into that can result in you missing out on many things in life. When you sleep in, rather than helping yourself rest better, you usually end up oversleeping which can actually leave you feeling even more tired. As well, if you are sleeping in on days where you have to be somewhere by a specific time, you are also sleeping during time that could be used preparing your mind, body, and emotions for the day.

Rather than sleeping in as long as you possibly can, get into the habit of waking up and engaging in a positive morning routine that allows you to completely prepare for your day in every way possible. This way, you are well rested, energized, and ready to face the day ahead of you.

Leaving Late

While waking up at a reasonable hour can help offset tardiness, there are many other reasons why you may be leaving late and, thus, arriving at appointments late, too. A lack of punctuality is something that can increase your own stress, while also pushing off any possible opportunities you may have access to because you are showing people that you do not care enough to take advantage of them. Learning how to leave on time and show up on time is a great way to take a load of stress off of your own mind while also proving to people that you are reliable and that you can handle any opportunity handed to you.

Since there are so many reasons why you might be tardy, it is a good idea to look into your own tendency of being late and discover what habits may be contributing to your lateness. This way, you can target your own habits and create solutions that will help you show up on time more often.

Relying On Temptations

Temptations are something we often put in our lives in an effort to make life easier for ourselves when, in reality, all we end up doing is making life harder. While relying on temptations to "save time" or for those "just in case" moments may seem ideal, the more likely reality is that they become crutches and we find ourselves actually sticking to convenient yet bad habits, rather than putting in the effort to achieve our desired habits. A great example of this would be buying convenience meal items for those nights where you may not feel like cooking. This may seem ideal, but what often ends up happening is that you rely on them more and more until you are no longer preparing healthy, homemade meals for yourself.

Rather than relying on unhealthy or less than ideal crutches as a way to help you get through times where you may not want to put the effort in, find healthier and simpler alternatives that will continue to help you get to your desired goal. For example, while purchasing convenience meals may not be a good habit to get into, meal prepping so that you have healthy meals made in advanced might be. The less you can rely on temptations, or keep them around as a backup option, the more likely you will be to stay on track with what you truly desire in your life.

Saying "I'll Do It Later"

Putting things off is about as bad as being perpetually late for everything in life. When you continue to put things off by saying, "I'll do it later," what ends up happening is you never actually get around to doing what you said you were going to do. As they say, "later never comes." Instead of waiting for later to never come, consider getting out of this habit by either shifting your language or shifting your follow up.

In situations where you do not actually want to do something, and you have no need to do it, rather than saying, "I'll do it later," try saying, "it is not a priority to me right now." This way, you can stop letting it nag at you and you can be honest about how you feel and what you need.

In situations where you do actually want to do something, or you need to do something, rather than saying, "I'll do it later" make actual plans for when you are going to do it and then put those plans down in your agenda. This way, rather than putting it off you are scheduling a specific time for when things are going to happen, and they are far more likely to get done.

Not Taking Your Wellbeing Seriously

Many of us are in the habit of neglecting our health to the point where it is somewhat of a punchline in a societal joke. With that being said, not taking your wellbeing seriously can lead to you experiencing incredibly ill health, which can lead to you not being able to achieve *any* goals, even your basic ones. You must get beyond the habits that keep you contributing to your ill health and begin taking your health seriously by adopting new, healthier habits that are going to support your wellbeing.

When it comes to how you take care of yourself, it can take quite a while to break down any bad habits you may be carrying, especially if you have many bad habits surrounding caring for yourself. It can be helpful to start tackling them one at a time and aiming for continuous improvement rather than immediate perfection. This way, you can take some of the pressure off of yourself, making it easier for you to do better and better over time.

Spreading Negativity

Another bad habit that you need to break, if you have it, is spreading negativity. Negativity can be spread by choosing to think negative or unhelpful thoughts, through gossiping, through saying rude, hurtful, or unhelpful things, and through otherwise choosing to spread negativity around between yourself and others. Spreading negativity only breeds more negativity, as it leads to you creating more reasons to be grumpy, pessimistic, or frustrated, rather than positive and supportive.

Instead of spreading negativity around, get into the habit of saying positive things to yourself and others, and staying quiet when you have nothing kind or positive to say. This way, you are spreading around positivity, and, as a result, you are attracting more positivity into your life. This is a great way to improve your mindset and open yourself up to the potential of new opportunities.

Conclusion

Thank you so much for reading *EMPOWERING HABITS!* This book was designed to help you understand habits and navigate them more effectively so that you can easily achieve your goals. In order to effectively achieve your goals, you need to understand the anatomy of a habit, the method for creating and changing habits, and the process for breaking bad habits.

I hope that after reading this book, you are feeling confident in all of this and more, as I truly believe that following the science of habits is key when it comes to achieving all of the lofty goals you set for yourself. The more you can embrace the power of your habits and leverage them to your advantage, the more likely you will be to reach all of your lofty goals and enjoy the life that you dream of having. In fact, it is my firm belief that this is the main difference between people who achieve their goals and people who don't.

Whenever it comes to achieving what you desire in life, especially when you desire big things, it can be helpful to work *with* your nature, rather than against it. In fact, in anything you do in life, it can be helpful to understand and work with your nature rather than against it, as this is often the most effective way for you to achieve a greater level of success in your life. After all, why put all of the work into trying to swim upstream against your natural current when, instead, you could subtly shift the flow of your current and achieve what you desire with greater success and ease?

After reading this book, I hope that you continue to learn about habits and how they work, and that you begin doing a deep exploration into your own habits and how they have been affecting you in your life. The more effectively you can begin to understand and navigate your habits, the more you will find yourself breaking down any habits that are no longer serving you and creating ones that help you make your way toward your goals.

It is important that you remember that no matter how long it has been since you have broken down an old goal or replaced it with a new one, there is always going to be the potential for you to slip back into old patterns. For that reason, you should always take the time to be mindful of your habits and what you are doing so that you can prevent yourself from slipping into old patterns and losing all of your progress. In fact, it may even be helpful for you to develop a habit of reviewing your habits at a set time every week, month, or year. The better you can navigate your new habits and remain mindful, the more likely you will be to achieve your desired results in your life.

The process of self-improvement, especially as far as our nature is concerned, truly is a lifelong process that we will need to continue to address and nurture over time. The more effective you are at taking this on as a lifelong journey and embracing each step of it without rushing to the "finish line," the more likely you will be to see great improvements. The goal is always to continue improving and never to be perfect. If you can embrace this goal, you will fulfill every single other goal you ever set for yourself. That, my friend, is the secret to success.

Before you go, I ask that you please take a moment to review *EMPOWERING HABITS: How to Acquire Habits That Will Lead You To Quickly Reach Your Goals* on Amazon Kindle. Your honest feedback would be greatly appreciated as it will allow me to continue to create powerful books to support you with improving your life, which, by the way, is one of my personal goals in life.

Thank you, and best of luck!

CPSIA information can be obtained
at www.ICGtesting.com
Printed in the USA
BVHW071030071220
595086BV00003B/341